DISCUSSIONS
A-Z
ADVANCED

A resource book of speaking activities

Adrian Wallwork

CAMBRIDGE
UNIVERSITY PRESS

PUBLISHED BY THE PRESS SYNDICATE OF THE UNIVERSITY OF CAMBRIDGE
The Pitt Building, Trumpington Street, Cambridge, United Kingdom

CAMBRIDGE UNIVERSITY PRESS
The Edinburgh Building, Cambridge CB2 2RU, UK
40 West 20th Street, New York, NY 10011–4211, USA
477 Williamstown Road, Port Melbourne, VIC 3207, Australia
Ruiz de Alarcón 13, 28014 Madrid, Spain
Dock House, The Waterfront, Cape Town 8001, South Africa

http://www.cambridge.org

First published 1997
Ninth printing 2003

Printed in Malaysia

A catalogue for this book is available from the British Library

ISBN 0 521 55979 0

Contents

Acknowledgements

I would like to thank above all Angie Graham for getting this project started and for all her subsequent advice. Thanks also to my father, Basil Wallwork, for doing a lot of the legwork and dogwork and for passing on to me his interest in words; to Andreina Marchesi and Tommaso for being a constant source of inspiration; to the many students who were guinea pigs for my ideas; to Francesco Oriolo for his immense knowledge and wit; to LIST SpA for letting me use their equipment; to International House in Pisa, in particular Chris Powell, Lynne Graziani and Antonia Clare; to Tau Pei Lin, Honor Routledge and Marcheline Frontini for their voices an ideas; to Robin Routledge for reading the early proofs; to my American, Dutch, South African and Ugandan neighbours for access to their brains and book shelves; and to Lindsay White for help and patience in the early stages.

I would also like to thank the following people at Cambridge University Press who suffered a lot of burning e-mails and faxes: Jeanne McCarten, Geraldine Mark, Nóirín Burke and Isabella Wigan. Thanks also to James Richardson, who produced the recordings, for being amazingly patient. I would also like to thank Felicity Currie for providing the listening extract of old English on p. 24.

Particular thanks are due to the following institutions and teachers for their help in testing the material and for the invaluable feedback which they provided: Jonathan Beesley, The British Council, Kuala Lumpur; Chris Evenden, Centro-Británico-Centro Español, Oviedo, Spain; Bob Hastings, Eurolingua, Córdoba, Spain; Sue Fraser, IALS, Edinburgh; Elizabeth McCallan, Executive Language Services, Paris, France; Sean Power, ELCRA Bell, Geneva; Tony Robinson, Eurocentres, Cambridge; Zofia Bernacka-Wos, Poland.

Possibly my greatest thanks should go to the authors of the 200 or so books that I read while preparing this book and its accompanying volume. I would particularly like to thank the following sources which provided me with a wealth of ideas: *Time* magazine, *The Sunday Times*, *The Times*, R. Ash: *The Top 10 of Everything*, *The Oxford English Dictionary*, *The Penguin Thesaurus*, *Webster's New World Dictionary* (third college edition), C. Wade and C. Travis: *Psychology*.

The author and publisher are grateful to the following for permission to use copyright material in *Discussions A–Z Advanced*. While every effort has been made, it has not been possible to identify the sources of all the material used and in such cases the publishers would welcome information from the copyright owners: Mel Smith and Griff Rhys-Jones for the extract on p. 9 from *The Smith and Jones World Atlas*; Laurence Pollinger Ltd. for the extract on p. 9 from the *Letters of Scott Fitzgerald* (UK and Commonwealth rights); US and Canada rights to the extract on p. 9 exerpted with permission of Scribner, a Division of Simon & Schuster from *F. Scott Fitzgerald – A Life in Letters* by Matthew J. Bruccoli. Copyright © 1994 by the Trustees under Agreement dated 3rd July, 1995 created by Frances Scott Fitzgerald Smith; Reed Books (UK and Common-wealth rights) and Simon & Schuster (US and Canada rights) for the extract on p. 11 from *How to Win Friends and Influence People* by Dale Carnegie; Virgin WH Allen for the extract on p. 11 from *The Art of Living* by Princess Beris Kandaouroff; HarperCollins Publishers for the extracts on pp. 16 and 76 from *Keywords*, the extract on p. 93 from *The Book of Tests* by M. Nathenson and the extract on p. 29 from *Psychology*, 2nd ed. by Carole Wade and Carol Travis; Ancient Art & Architecture Collection for the photo (Mereworth House) on p. 17;

Popperfoto for the photos (The Beatles, Johann Sebastian Bach) on p. 17 and p. 97; Prentice-Hall for the extract on p. 17 from *SOCIOLOGY Understanding Society*; the estate of G.L. Brook for the extracts on pp. 25 and 105 from *An Introduction to Old English* by G.L. Brook; Oxford University Press for the extracts on pp. 28 and 29 from *Phobia – the Facts* by D. Goodwin; the University of Natal for the extract on p. 31 from *Focus*, 1994, Vol. 5, no. 4; Plenum Publishing Corporation for the extract on p. 32 from *Sex Roles*, Vol. 23; Simon & Schuster for the extract on p. 33 from *I've done so well – Why do I feel so bad?* by Celia Hallas and Roberta Matteson; The Reader's Digest Association Ltd. for the extract on p. 35 from *The Right Word at the Right Time* © 1995; Panos Pictures for the photos on pp. 39 and 99; Funk & Wagnalls Corporation for the information on p. 39 from *The World Almanac and Book of Facts*; Express Enterprises for the extract on p. 41 from the *Sunday Express*, 19 July 1992; Express Newspapers plc for the photo on p. 41; Open University Press for the extract on p. 42 from *The Skilful Mind* by A. Gellatly; Prion for the extract on p. 47 from *Mindwatching* by H. & M. Eysenck; Little Brown (UK) Ltd. for the extract on p. 47 from *Book of Childcare* by H. Jolly; the British Association of Non-Parents for the extracts on pp. 48 and 49 from their leaflet *No Regrets (The Case for Remaining Childless)*; the British Agencies for Adoption and Fostering (BAAF) for the extract on p. 50 from their leaflet; Souvenir Press Ltd. for the illustrations from *Signs Make Sense* by C. Smith on p. 55; Penguin UK for the extract on p. 58 from *Conceptual Blockbusting* by James L. Adams (UK and Commonwealth rights) and the extracts on pp. 85 and 104 from *Sociolinguistics* by Peter Trudgill; Addison-Wesley for the extract on p. 58 from *Conceptual Blockbusting* by James L. Adams (US and Canada rights); Routledge for the extract on p. 65 from *Pros and Cons* by M. D. Jackson; National Magazine Company for the extract on p. 67 from *Cosmopolitan* magazine; Omnibus Press for the extract on p. 69 from *Bob Dylan in his own words*; Econ for the extract on p. 71 from *The Personality Test* by Peter Lauster; British Telecommunications plc for the extracts and illustrations on pp. 72, 73 and 75 from their booklet *The Language of Success*; School of Living for the extract on p. 77 from *Go Ahead and Live* by Mildred J. Loomis; the Equal Opportunities Commission for the extract on p. 78 from *The Inequality Gap*; the Academic Press for the definitions on p. 81 from the *Academic Press Dictionary of Science and Technology*; Victor Gollancz and Virginia Kidd Literary Agency for the extract on p. 83 from *The Dispossessed* by Ursula Le Guin; MIT Press for the extracts on pp. 84 and 104 from *Style in Language* by T.A. Sebeok; Piatkus Books and Dr Lillian Glass for the extract on p. 86 from *Confident Conversation* by Dr Lillian Glass; Stanley Thornes for the extract on p. 87 from *Teaching Children to Think* by Robert Fisher; W.W. Norton & Company for the extract on p. 89 from Robert Adams' trans-lation of *Utopia* by Sir Thomas More; Brooks/Cole Publishing Company for the extract on p. 95 from *Social Psychology on the 80s* by Deaux/ Wrightsman; WWF UK for the extract on p. 99 from *The WWF Environment Handbook;* Mary Evans Picture Library for the photos (UFO and When Martians landed) on p. 111; Planet Earth Pictures for the photos (satellite, cluster of colliding galaxy, Vlar telescope, pace telescope) on p. 111.

Illustrations by Graham Cox: pp. 29, 33, 63, 65, 85, 95; Chris Pavely: pp. 13, 55, 57, 61, 81; Graham Puckett: pp. 33 (top), 37 (bottom); David Seabourne and Tommaso Wallwork: p. 83; Peter Seabourne: pp. 49, 51; Gary Wing: pp. 17, 37 (top), 45, 67, 71, 77, 109. Page layout by David Seabourne.

Introduction

Summary for those in a hurry

- **Structure:** There are 26 topic-related units – one for each letter of the alphabet. Topics overlap between units, which means that you can pass from one unit to another, and so give your students a sense of thematic continuity.
- **Level and use:** Use the book both for back-up material to your coursebook, or independently as the basis of a conversation course and try it with lower levels as well.
- **Where to begin:** If your class is not familiar with discussion activities, the best entry point is **Talk** which has several activities to get students thinking about how to conduct a discussion. Otherwise start with the warm-ups from **Advice** or **Zodiac**.
- **Subject and Links index:** Use the subject index to decide what exercises to use. This index is designed to help you locate exercises which will tie in with your coursebook; many unit titles and headings of typical upper level coursebooks are covered in this index. You can use the links index to plan a conversation course – it tells you the various connections among units.
- **Choosing exercises:** Don't feel you have to do every exercise from every unit. Combine exercises from various units as you choose both from this book and from *Discussions A–Z Intermediate*. Don't follow the order of the exercises unless you want to (or unless advised in the teacher's notes).
- **Timing:** Exercises vary in length from five to about ninety minutes depending on your students' level and interest in the topic. Don't impose any rigorous time limits unless you have to, but don't persevere with a discussion that's getting nowhere. However, it is important that students feel they've completed an exercise and been linguistically productive in the process.
- **Personalisation:** Try and relate exercises to current events and things relevant to your own students' lives.
- **Taboo:** Some topics may be sensitive for your students – they are marked with a ☝. Don't let this put you off doing them unless you're sure they will react badly. If you think they might, make sure you have back-up material ready (for example, exercises from the **Quizzes** unit).
- **Discussion groups:** Most of the discussion exercises work best in pairs or small groups. Explain to students that you won't interrupt them while they talk (unless you notice them repeatedly making the same mistake), but that you'll note down mistakes they make for analysis at a later point. In any case, before embarking on an exercise you should anticipate any vocabulary and grammar problems that are likely to arise, and revise these beforehand if necessary. With more reticent classes you may need to drill or feed them with relevant structures useful for the specific discussion task.

- **Other uses:** Don't think that you have to use this book just for discussions. Some ideas could lead you on to other areas: vocabulary, grammar, composition writing etc.
- **Flexibility:** Be flexible. Choose your own path through the book. Use the link cross references on the teacher's pages to guide you. Select and adapt the tasks to suit your students' needs. Rework the exercises or use them as models for your own ideas.
- **Comments:** Please write to me at Cambridge, or e-mail me (adrian@list.it) and let me know your opinions and criticisms on the book.

Speaking

Most exercises on the student's page consist of a set of questions to discuss. When these questions are preceded by an introductory reading passage they should not be treated as comprehension questions but as a springboard to discussion. If you see no logical ordering in the numbering of the questions let students read all the questions, and then just select the ones they wish to discuss. Alternatively divide students into small groups and ask them to discuss, say, only the first five of ten questions. Those who finish their discussion quickly can be asked to move on to the other questions, whilst the more loquacious groups are given enough time to finish their debates.

Don't let students think they have to stick to answering the questions directly. Let them float around the questions and bring in their own ideas.

Questions not discussed in the lesson can be set as titles for compositions for homework; or summaries can be made of those questions that were in fact answered during the lesson.

Reading

Most of the texts are authentic and come from a variety of sources; some have been condensed or slightly modified. They have been kept deliberately short and are not designed for developing specific reading skills. Encourage students to guess:

- where the texts come from – newspapers, scientific journals, women's magazines, letters, interviews, literary works (for sources see p.4)
- why they were written – to inform, instruct, convince, advise, shock, amuse, deceive
- who they were written for – age group, sex, nationality, specialist, casual reader
- when they were written (where applicable)
  Although the aim of the text is not to act as a comprehension exercise, students should obviously understand most of what they read. Before photocopying, underline in pencil any parts that you feel are essential for an understanding of the text. Check the meaning of these before going on to look at the text in more detail.

Introduction

Depending on the type of text as a written follow-up, students can:

- rewrite the text from a different point of view.
- imagine and recount what happened either before or after the event described in the text. Alternatively they write up an interview with the people mentioned in the text. This interview could even take place ten years later, to find out their new situations or feelings.
- summarise the text, or simply delete any words or phrases that they consider could be redundant.

Listening

The listening exercises vary in level to a much greater extent than in the reading and speaking exercises and can be used with a good range of classes. These exercise are also designed to provide information and provoke discussion but some listenings can also be used as free-standing exercises to improve listening skills.

None of the listenings are referred to on the student's pages, so you should give clear instructions for the exercises. You will also need to dictate the comprehension questions, or write them on the board for students to copy. Feel free to adapt the questions or invent your own to suit the level or interests of your students. Pre-teach any essential vocabulary that has not already come up during the preceding discussion exercise.

Some listening exercises feature native speakers doing the exercise on the student's page. Ask students to read all the questions but without answering them. Then get them to listen to the first two speakers. On the first listening they identify which point is being discussed. After the second listening elicit the structures and vocabulary used – this will then serve as a basis for the students' own discussions. The other speakers can then be used at the end of the exercise, purely as a comprehension test.

Culture and maturity

I am English, but you will notice that there is a considerable American input too. Most of the subjects covered thus reflect a fairly liberal Anglo-Saxon background, and my age (born 1959). Some subjects may encroach on taboo areas in your students culture and you should take care to consult students in advance about any potentially delicate topics where they might feel embarrassed or exposed. A very simple way to check possible problems areas, is to give each student a copy of the **subject index** (page 112) and get them to tick any subjects they would feel uneasy about. I would also get them to write their name, so that you know exactly who has problems with what. This means that such subjects could be discussed in such people's absence. This is a good introductory exercise in itself, and combined with the **Talk** unit, should get your students analysing what verbal communication is all about. Also, check out any extreme or prejudiced opinions your students may have, whilst these could actually be used to good effect (as a kind of devil's advocate), they might upset other students.

Don't attempt subjects that are simply outside the realm of your students' experience – no amount of imagination is going to be able to surmount the problem. But if you ask them to pretend to be part of a doctors' ethics committee, obviously they can't be expected to know what a real doctor would do, but that shouldn't stop them saying what they would do if they were in such a position.

If you do unwittingly embark on an exercise which students find too difficult or embarrassing, or which promotes little more than uneasy silence, just abandon it – but try and predict such events and have back-up exercises at the ready. Feel free just to ignore some exercises completely, but tell students that the nature of the book is not to cover every exercise systematically and in order. You'll soon learn the types of exercises that will go down well with your students. I would suggest letting the *students* decide which exercises they want to do.

Most exercises in this book have been designed to be very flexible, and an exercise that might appear to be too difficult or delicate can often be adapted to suit your students' needs. In countries where students are likely to seize on a writing exercise, however brief the writing, and use it as a substitute for speaking rather than a prelude to it, you may need to rethink some of the exercise instructions. For example, in one exercise students are asked to rate some moral values (**Values**) from one to five according to unacceptability. Don't let them get hold of their pen and merely write numbers, but give them clear cut instructions to which they can't avoid talking: 'Look at the situations below and decide if they are wrong. If they are wrong, how wrong are they? Tell your partner what you think and give reasons for your opinion'. (I am indebted to Jonathan Beesley of the British Council in Kuala Lumpur for these and other suggestions.)

If you feel students cannot cope with a certain exercise because they wouldn't know what to say, then you might have to provide them with a concrete stimulus. For example, students are asked to answer the question 'What difficulties do homeless people have?' If they have difficulty in putting themselves in other people's shoes, you could put them into pairs – one journalist and one homeless person and give them role cards. On the journalist's card you specify areas to ask questions about (e.g. sleep, food, clothes, money, friends, consideration of and by others – but in a little more detail than this). On the homeless person's card put information that could answer such questions (e.g. sleep under a bridge, at the station, hospice, etc.). Alternatively, in pairs again, they imagine they are both homeless people, but from two different parts of the world (e.g. New York and Calcutta). By giving them such obvious differences (climate, lifestyle, culture), you get them focusing their ideas more clearly. This principle can be applied to many of the exercises.

Introduction

How to conduct a discussion

The word 'discuss' originally meant to 'cut' with a similar origin as 'dissect'. This meaning, along with its current use of 'examining the pros and cons' gives a good idea of what a discussion is all about, i.e. a dissection of an argument into various parts for analysis, followed by a reassembling of all the relevant elements to a draw a conclusion from the whole. *Discussions A–Z* is based on this principle.

One problem with **question answering** is that without some coaching on how to answer questions, students may simply answer 'yes', 'no', 'it depends' etc., and then move on to the next question. Many of the questions in this book have been formulated so that they avoid a simple 'yes/no' answer. Others are designed to be deliberately provocative.

Consider the following case. Students are asked whether it should be up to the government or the people to decide on where people can smoke. If students simply answer 'the government' or 'the people', there won't be much to discuss.

Alternatively, students (either alone or in groups) should first write down a set of related questions, e.g. Where are smokers free to smoke now? Why do we need to change this? Why do we need a law to tell us we can't smoke in certain places? Who would object to anti-smoking legislature? Who would benefit? What should be done with offenders? etc. The process of formulating and answering these types of questions will get the students really thinking, and along with some examples from their own personal experience, should lead to intense language production.

The same kind of approach can be used for **brainstorming**. Suppose you're brainstorming the students on the ideal qualities of a judge. Without any prior instruction, most people will come up with personality characteristics such as intelligent, well-balanced, rational, experienced – which is fine. But it would be more productive if students first wrote down a set of questions related to judges: Why do we need judges? What is a judge? How old should he be? Even the phrasing of questions can be indicative of how we see a judge – why do we refer to a judge as 'he' and not 'she'? Are men more rational, and therefore better judges than women, and why is it that there are so few female judges? You should add other, less orthodox questions, to provoke your students into thinking about other aspects of being a judge, e.g. how relevant are race, height and physical appearance, hobbies etc.? Students may think that the height of a judge is totally irrelevant; this is probably true (though research has shown that there is a link between height and intelligence), but

often by saying what is not important we get a clearer idea of what is important. As a follow-up activity students could design a training course for judges.

Now let us see how we can apply the same approach to problem-solving activities. Suppose your students are part of a government board which gives funding to scientific research projects. Their task is to decide which one of the following projects to give money to: (1) a group of marine archaeologists who have found Atlantis; (2) some alchemists who have found a way to convert the Grand Canyon into gold; and (3) some genetic engineers who have developed a way to produce square fruit. In order to generate a valuable discussion students should begin by writing down a series of related questions: Why did the scientists involved propose the projects? Is there a real need for such a project? Is it practical? Do we have the necessary technology to carry it out? Should such projects be funded by the government or by private enterprise? Who would benefit and why? etc. Then, when they are into their discussion, they should try and extend their arguments and reasoning and see where it takes them.

For example, a discussion on Atlantis might, if pre-questions have been written, lead naturally into an analysis of what we can learn from history, how and why legends arise, why archaeology of any kind is important, what things we can learn from past civilisations, how our past affects the present, etc.

In summary, this approach to discussion involves:
- A pre-discussion activity where students, either in groups or individually, write down related questions, some of which you, the teacher, can feed.
- A discussion initiated by answering such questions, and if possible, drawing on students' own personal experiences.
- The logical or illogical extension of ideas brought up by the discussion.
- A round-up of conclusions involving cross-group questioning followed by whole class feedback.
- A written summary for consolidation.

The result is obviously a much fuller and productive discussion, in which you have more time to note down any recurrent mistakes, and students to let themselves go and practise their English. Nor are the benefits solely linguistic: there is a great deal of satisfaction in having your mind stretched and producing interesting and often unexpected ideas and results.

Advice

Warm-up

- This exercise can be used as a first lesson with a new group.
- In a monolingual class tell your students (in groups) to discuss and write down some advice for foreigners (e.g. you) about living and surviving in their country. Some should be real advice and some should be invented. They then read out their advice and you have to tell them whether you think it is real advice or invented – this will obviously work particularly well if you really have just arrived in their country. Then you do the same to them, i.e. give them advice about your country and they have to identify from what you say whether the advice is real or invented. If this is your first lesson they can also identify which country you are from.
- As a follow-up reading exercise, photocopy the introduction from a tourist guide (written in English, e.g. *The Rough Guide*) where it talks about the general characteristics of the people of your host country. Students read the extract and then discuss, initially in groups and then with you, whether they agree with what the guide says.
- In a multilingual class, before students have had the chance to get to know each other and discover where they come from, tell them to write some advice for visitors to their country (only true information). In groups they then read out their advice and the other students have to guess their country of origin.

Writing

- Students imagine a foreigner has come to their country. They are in three different historical periods: stone age, middle ages and 19th century. Their task is to write down two or three pieces of advice for each period that they would give to this imaginary foreigner. In groups they then read out at random the pieces of advice. The others have to decide which period the advice refers to and whether they agree with it or not.

1 Tips for tourists

- Students first identify the maps and flags of the various countries shown in the illustrations. Get feedback and give answers.

🔑 **a** *Australia* **b** *Saudi Arabia* **c** *Kenya* **d** *Norway* **e** *Peru* **f** *USA* **g** *Malaysia* **h** *Japan* **i** *Switzerland* **j** *Denmark*

- Students now read the advice for tourists and in groups identify which country is being referred to (note that there are three extra countries illustrated). Give answers.

🔑 **1** *Australia* **2** *Saudi Arabia* **3** *Japan* **4** *Peru* **5** *Norway (Oslo)* **6** *USA* **7** *Kenya*

- Finally, students discuss whether they have already visited or would like to visit those countries.

2 Good advice?

- Tell students to read the extracts and in groups to work out where the passages might have come from (book, magazine, play, etc.), who wrote them, who they were for, and when they were written. Get feedback and give them the information below. NB If the Shakespeare extract is too difficult just use the Fitzgerald one.

ⓘ The first advice is from a letter written in 1933 by Scott Fitzgerald (author of *The Great Gatsby*) to his 12-year-old daughter who was away at school. The second is from Shakespeare's Hamlet and is Polonius's advice to his son Laertes before Laertes departs for France. Tell students that even most native speakers find Shakespeare's English hard to understand without a little practice. Inform students that *thee/thou* = you, *thy/thine* = your.

- Now ask them to decide whether the advice is good.
- Finally, do the listening.

Listening

- Students hear some possible modern interpretations of six of the seven extracts from Polonius's speech. Their task is to match the version with the original.

🔑 **1**c **2**a **3**e **4**f **5**b **6**g

💻 1 Basically I suppose it means um, well don't get into arguments, but if you do, make sure that the person you're arguing with knows who they're dealing with.

2 I'm not sure em, something like, don't say what you're thinking and think hard before you do anything; is that it?

3 Buy expensive but not ostentatious clothes as people often judge you on the way you look; not sure I agree with that one.

4 Don't give or ask for money: one, you might lose the money or your friend, and two you might not keep within your budget.

5 Don't let go of loyal friends – too right.

6 Actually this is pretty much my motto: be true to yourself, if you do, you will be sincere with everybody else.

Advice

1 Tips for tourists

1 Think before you go. Convicts used to beg to be executed rather than exiled to this English-speaking island.

2 When eating in someone's home: Eat only with your right hand. Do not sit with the soles of your feet facing anyone. Do not ask for alcohol.

3 Don't expect to find a husband or wife in this Eastern country. Of all the peoples of the world, they are the least inclined to marry foreigners. Don't worry about being mugged. There is very little violent crime here compared with other advanced countries.

4 Ride on the highest standard gauge railway in the world, at 15,801 ft. Avoid the Amazon jungle – it is said to contain tribes of cannibals and head-shrinkers.

5 Visit this European capital, the fourth largest city in the world in size, with a population of less than half a million. This is the result of a decision in 1948 to simply make it 27 times larger. Most of the city is forest and park.

6 Respect the flag. It must not be left in the dark or get wet or touch the ground. Be careful of the phone. Although there are as many as 550 million calls every day, they may be monitored. Do not be lured into marriage. There are half as many divorces as marriages.

7 Enjoy the wildlife. Visit the Great Rift Valley, where some anthropologists believe the human race began. This country has the world's highest birth rate and rape rate, and the lowest rates for suicide and car accident deaths.

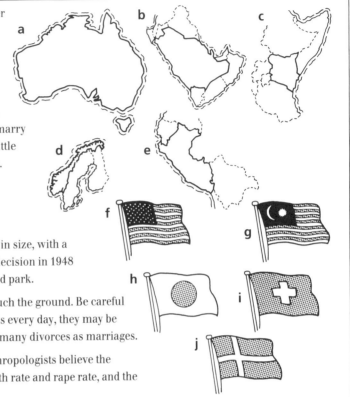

2 Good advice?

Things to worry about:
Worry about courage. Worry about cleanliness.
Worry about efficiency. Worry about horsemanship ...

Things not to worry about:
Don't worry about popular opinion.
Don't worry about dolls.
Don't worry about the past.
Don't worry about the future.
Don't worry about growing up.
Don't worry about anyone getting ahead of you.
Don't worry about triumph.
Don't worry about failure unless it comes through your own fault ...
Don't worry about parents.
Don't worry about boys.
Don't worry about disappointments.
Don't worry about pleasures.
Don't worry about satisfactions ...

Give thy thoughts no tongue,
Nor any unproportion'd thought his act.
Be thou familiar, but by no means vulgar. (a)
Those friends thou hast, and their adoption tried,
Grapple them to thy soul with hoops of steel; (b)
Beware of entrance to a quarrel; but, being in,
Bear't that th'opposed may beware of thee. (c)
Give every man thy ear, but few thy voice;
Take each man's censure, but reserve thy judgment. (d)
Costly thy habit as thy purse can buy,
But not express'd in fancy; rich, not gaudy;
For the apparel oft proclaims the man; (e)
Neither a borrower nor a lender be;
For loan oft loses both itself and friend,
And borrowing dulls the edge of husbandry. (f)
This above all — to thine own self be true,
And it must follow, as the night the day,
Thou canst not then be false to any man. (g)

Advice

3 How to win friends

- Before reading the text, ask students to discuss in groups some of the best ways to win and keep friends.
- Tell students that there are 12 pieces of advice, on winning and keeping friends, from two very different books: one is called *The art of living* by someone with the unlikely name of Princess Beris Kandaouroff (basically a book on social etiquette), the other is one of the world's most successful business books, called *How to win friends and influence people* by Dale Carnegie (originally published in 1936, with nearly ten million copies now sold).
- Students' initial task is to decide which pieces go with which book. However, it will soon become apparent that most pieces could fit both books, and the prime aim should be to discuss whether the advice is good or not. Students may like to add some more of their own rules of friendship.

🔑 *Carnegie:* **1–6**: *Beris:* **7–12**. *Don't tell students beforehand that one half is from one book and the other is from the other book.*

Follow-up
- Is it possible to have a real friendship with someone of the opposite sex? Is it true that the older you get, the more difficult it is to make friends?

4 Problems pages

- Explain what a problem page is (generally a page in a woman's magazine where readers write in with problems, which are then answered by an expert). Brainstorm students on the kinds of problems likely to be found on such pages and write a list on the board (adding any topics from the letters in the exercise that students don't think of). Students read the letters and match them with topics from the list. In groups students discuss what advice they'd give these readers.

Listening
- Students hear some advice/opinions on the letters. They identify which answer goes with which problem, and then discuss the opinions.

🔑 *1E* *2A* *3C* *4B* *5B* *6C* *7E* *8D*

📼 1 It sounds to me as if she basically doesn't accept herself. She should stop thinking about altering her appearance and think more about her attitude to herself and her approach to other people. Maybe she should seek professional advice, first from her doctor and then from a psychotherapist. But I do feel sorry for her.

2 She seems to be trying to make a connection between the gypsy's curse and what happened later. There's no doubt that she's been very unlucky, but the only way to break the chain is to get support from the rest of her family and to think positively. I reckon when people get into the state of mind she's in, they are almost encouraging, so to speak, negative things to happen. She really needs to break the vicious circle she seems to have got herself in.

3 These days I think people are judged more on their merits than on their accent, and I think she should realise that it's probably more of a problem for her than for the people who listen to her. Britain certainly is a class conscious society, but things are changing, and anyway who wants to speak like the Queen?

4 Anyone who's thinking of having a child at that age in my opinion is thoroughly selfish. It seems to me that scientists and doctors are really in some kind of perverse competition to see whose patient can deliver a baby at the oldest age possible. Science is enabling us to do things, that quite frankly, it would be better if we couldn't do. Why don't these people think more about the poor children they are going to have, who are going to grow up with what looks more like grandparents than parents?

5 Why not? I mean we live far longer these days anyway, so it's not as if the child is going to miss out. And why always look at it from the child's point of view? And anyway at least she or he is going to have mature, economically stable parents to be looked after by.

6 I know exactly what she means. The kids at my school always used to tease me for the way I spoke, and I actually ended up asking my parents to give me elocution lessons. They refused, so I began to watch loads of old black and white films and tried to imitate the way the rich ladies spoke.

7 This woman needs her head seeing to. Does she realise how many women would give their left arm, so to speak, to look like her?

8 I feel terribly sorry that we live in a society that cannot accept the inconvenience of having an old person in their house – and we're not talking about any old person, but a member of one's own family. There are still some tribes where the oldest member is considered to be the wisest, and I think that people forget that even in this age of advanced technology we can still learn a lot from the older members of our society. I remember that my old granny got shoved in an old people's home, but she kept ringing up for a taxi to take her home. It was so sad. And they lose their spirit so quickly in those places. They're like waiting rooms for a cemetery. Horrible. I'd tell her to emigrate to Australia and live with her son.

Advice

3 How to win friends

1 Become genuinely interested in other people.

2 Smile.

3 Remember that someone's name is to them the sweetest and most important sound in any language.

4 Be a good listener. Encourage others to talk about themselves.

5 Talk in terms of the other person's interest.

6 Make the other person feel important – and do it sincerely.

7 Friends are like flowers.

8 Don't expect too much from anybody. Take what they can give, and be prepared to be more generous in return.

9 Never give advice unless it's specifically asked for.

10 Never drop in unexpectedly.

11 Do not encourage your friends to tell you their troubles all the time.

12 Be unquestioningly loyal.

4 Problems pages

A A few years ago I had my hand read by a gypsy. She told me a lot of very detailed things, all of which were strikingly true. Then she asked me for a lot of money, about £10 I think, and although I had the money with me I refused to give it to her, telling her that I thought it was too much. She went on and on at me and in the end I gave her £1, at which point she made a very elaborate curse and ever since my life has been a total disaster. A month later my husband had a fatal car accident, then I lost my job and now I've lost my hearing in one ear. I'm desperate.

B I am 50, have recently remarried, and am madly in love with my new husband. It's his first marriage and he'd dearly love to have children. I am very tempted but my 30-year-old daughter from my first marriage says I'd be out of my mind. What do you think?

C I come from Newcastle and my accent is really getting me down, as my voice makes me feel inferior. The problem is that I married into a rather posh family, and I end up not talking at all so as not to get embarrassed. This of course gives an even worse impression so I feel even more depressed. Would elocution lessons help?

D I'm so unhappy. I'm only 68 but I'm stuck in this old people's home where most people are 10, 20 even 30 years older than me. I suffer from rheumatoid arthritis, yet with my drugs I can move around quite well. My brain is very alert and I feel like I'm in some dreadful prison. My only son lives in Australia. What can I do?

E Please don't think I'm vain but I do know that I'm extremely attractive and have a very good figure. The problem is people like to be seen with me, but they're not interested in getting to know me. I'm 23 and I've tried various ways of making myself look less attractive – wearing scruffy clothes, cutting my hair short – but none of them work. Should I have some cosmetic surgery done? I really need to be taken seriously by someone.

Body

Warm-up

- Brainstorm students on what they associate with the word 'body'. For example, the various sciences use the word in different ways: in **anatomy** it is the largest and most important part of any organ, whereas in **zoology** it is the trunk of an animal, excluding the head, limbs and tail; in **astronomy** it is a moon, planet, star or other heavenly body; in **graphics** they talk about the body of a text, as opposed to headlines, captions, etc.; and in **mechanical engineering** it is the part of a vehicle in which passengers ride or a load is carried.

1 Can you live without it?

- Students look at the illustration of the exterior part of the human body on their page. First check that they know the names of the parts of the body. Then get them to choose the three most essential parts; not only in a physical/utility sense but also in terms of how essential they are to one's sense of self. This is basically a prioritising exercise which should also include analysing what parts of our body we could manage without. You can extend this exercise by getting students to imagine how much they would insure various parts of their body for.
- Now get students to guess how much the interior parts weigh.

☛ *Weight in kilos: liver – 1.5, brain – 1.4 (male), 1.3 (female), lungs – 1.1 (total), heart – 0.3 (male), 0.26 (female), kidney – 0.3 (both).*

Follow-up

- Students draw a (humorous) version of the human body with improvements; they then compare and discuss their pictures. Alternatively, students discuss how they would improve the human body (e.g. ability to fly, removable and replaceable/regrowable parts, ability to see in the dark, extra arms and legs, eyes at the back of or on top of head). They then talk about the consequences of these changes (e.g. If we had eyes at the back of our heads we would have to change our hairstyle; I wish I could fly then I wouldn't have problems finding a parking space).

2 Body language

- Focus students' attention on the illustrations on their page, but without analysing each illustration individually. Brainstorm students on why we need body language – aren't words good enough? Then orient the discussion in terms of what they can do with their hands (e.g. beckon people, put them in their pockets), what they can't do (vulgar signs), how they show respect, when laughing is permissible and what it means, how to show approval, how they kiss each other when meeting, etc. This activity should be more interesting as a whole class activity, rather than in groups.

Listening

- Students hear two teachers discussing their teaching experiences around the world in relation to body language. Students may like to guess the answers to these questions before listening.

Questions: **1** What may smiling mean in Japan? **2** What things do men do in Italy that the speaker found strange? **3** What does the hand gesture the speaker refers to mean in Italy? **4** How should you point to someone in India? **5** How should you beckon someone in Korea?

☛ **1** *embarrassment* **2** *walking arm in arm, kissing* **3** *What do you mean? What's happening?* **4** *with chin* **5** *palm down*

- After the listening students get into pairs to describe the illustrations to each other. The other student has to guess which illustration is being described, and what the meaning is.
- Finally, get students to read the facts on their page. To make the exercise more interesting white out the numbers and other interesting information, and get students to fill in the gaps.

A ... and it was really embarrassing because winking means that you want a child to leave the room.

B That's, that's really odd. You know one of the most embarrassing experiences I had was when I first arrived in Japan. I had this all girl group, right, and I was telling them some stupid joke, I don't remember what it was now, anyway because they were all smiling I thought that not only were they understanding what I was saying but that they were also enjoying it too. But I discovered afterwards that the more they were smiling the more they were getting embarrassed. Anyway that was the last time I tried to be funny ...

A Yeah, well in Italy where I taught for a couple of years you can say and do almost anything.

B You know, whenever I've been in Italy on holiday I've always been struck by the way the men go around arm in arm, and they kiss each other when they meet.

A But did you notice how many gestures they use?

B Um.

A There's one hand gesture that means 'What on earth are you talking about?' or 'What's going on here?', a kind of incredulity sign; then there's one meaning that you're wanted on the phone, and ...

B Yeah, yeah, yeah, of course in Japan they don't use many hand gestures, in fact it seems to be like that pretty much all over the Far East. I know that in India they use their chin to point rather than their fingers; in Korea and I think Hong Kong too, if they want to beckon you they'll never use their finger, but their entire hand with the palm down.

A I think in the Middle East they never use their left hand at all.

B It, eh, must be a bit awkward if you're left-handed.

A Yeah, right.

1 Can you live without it?

2 Body language

People in Britain stand about 0.5 m away from a person in an intimate context, 0.5–1.5 m (family, friends), 3–4 m (others).

Tests have shown that people are more influenced by how people say something than what they say. For example, if someone says something friendly but with an air of superiority (not smiling, head raised, with a loud dominating voice), it is the attitude of superiority which will have the lasting effect, not the words themselves.

People form 90% of their opinion of someone in the first 90 seconds.

In a conversation, the speaker should look at his/her interlocutor about 40% of the time, while the listener should look 65% of the time. Direct one-to-one eye contact should last one and a half seconds.

Mothers touch their sons more than sons touch their mothers. Fathers touch their daughters more than they touch their sons.

The number of times people touch each other depends on where they were born. During a one-hour conversation between two people in a bar in Puerto Rico the number of touches was 180 (in Paris 110, in London 0!).

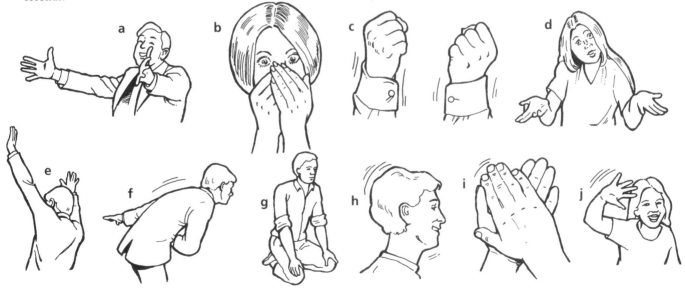

3 Medical ethics

This exercise touches on some sensitive issues.

- Get students to focus on the title **Medical ethics** and elicit explanations. Inform them that health service costs have become so expensive that it is becoming impossible to treat all cases and soon they will have to be ranked in order of importance. Doctors are having to weigh up the cost of the operation and the benefits to the patient in terms of quality and duration of life. Doctors faced with these choices give high priority to prenatal care, birth control and immunisation; organ transplants, cosmetic surgery and eating disorders get low priority.

- Before they read the seven cases, students imagine they are on the ethics committee of a hospital. An ethics committee is a group of people who have to decide what is 'morally' right to do in circumstances connected with a patient's health. In this case students have to prioritise the seven cases. They should go on the assumption that if an operation is needed, and it is not done now, the opportunity will not arise again (though they may find this an unrealistic constraint, it might happen in the future).

- I suggest two ways to approach this exercise. Give students a certain amount of money that they can spend (e.g. a total of $10 – obviously the total real cost would be several hundred thousand dollars.) Allocate a cost to each case. For example (1) $3 (2) $2 (3) $2 (4) $1 total (5) $1 total (6) $3 (7) $1. This means that the total cost will be greater than $10, i.e. students won't be able to treat all of the cases with the money they have. Alternatively, imagining that all of the cases have an equal cost, students select three to do, having first decided on some criteria for making this selection.

4 Out-of-body experiences

- Students read the text and discuss the questions in groups.

A 'rakehell' is a sorcerer or scoundrel.

Body

3   Medical ethics

1
> This man needs a heart transplant; he is very overweight. Heart transplants give a further life expectancy of around five years.

2
> This man needs a sex change. He has been waiting for five years for the operation and has attempted suicide on three occasions. Sex change operations are known to have an extremely high success rate, far higher than for any other surgical procedure.

3
> This father is the sole income provider for a wife and five children. He needs a coronary bypass, which stands a 90% chance of being completely successful.

4
> These five patients all need cataract operations. All have been waiting for over a year and all are unlikely to be able to do their current jobs if their eye problems are not resolved.

5
> These two 60-cigarettes-a-day smokers need operations to have malignant tumours removed. Their life expectancy is thought to be no more than six months.

6
> This two-month-old baby needs a heart and lung transplant. The surgery needed is so new that no-one knows the chances of the baby's survival.

7
> This 80-year-old lady has just had a very serious car crash, and is now in a coma in the emergency ward.

4   Out-of-body experiences

OOBEs (out-of-body experiences) work in two ways. First there are the experiences countless people have had of seeming to leave their body temporarily, either to visit the afterlife, as has been frequently reported in cases of people who have recovered from near-death, or simply to travel far from their physical bodies. Second there are instances of people appearing — miles away from where they actually are — in front of their friends or acquaintances.

In 1863 S.R.Wilmot sailed from England to rejoin his family in the United States. He shared a cabin with one William Tait. One night Wilmot 'saw' his wife, clad only in her nightie, enter the cabin, hesitate when she saw someone else there, and then conquer her shyness to come over to his bunk and kiss him.

It is not unnatural that spouses separated for a long time should have such visions. What startled Wilmot, however, was that in the morning Tait accused him of being a rakehell: he too had seen this scantily clad woman entering the cabin and behaving with a certain lack of decorum. To make the matter even odder, on his arrival in New York Wilmot was asked by his wife whether he remembered the 'visit'; she described exactly what had happened, and on subsequent questioning was able to give details of the general layout of the cabin.

1 What are the implications of being able to leave your body temporarily and visit the afterlife?

2 What benefits would there be of being able to be in two places at the same time, or of being able to materialise wherever you want? (And if you were the only person who was able to do this?)

3 Do you believe the story of Wilmot and his wife? Why? Why not?

4 Do you practise any activities such as yoga, transcendental meditation, hypnotism, etc.? If you don't, what do you think of people who do?

Class

(i) This unit covers the concept of class in many of its different meanings. There is no logical connection between exercises; they can all be used separately.

'Class' originally referred to the six divisions of people in the Roman constitution, which was then extended as a general term for a division or group. One of its main uses in England in the 17th century (it had been borrowed from Latin the century before) was connected with authoritative and scholarly study, and this sense of course remains today in terms of classes in schools, along with its other sense of ranking. Class with its social meaning really came into being in the Industrial Revolution, in which society was reorganised (1770–1840). Until that time, 'rank', 'estate' and 'order' had been used to express social position, and some snobs still refer (not always with tongue in cheek) to the 'lower orders'. At that time, people were born into a particular class and were stuck with it; social mobility was virtually unheard of. But our modern division into upper, middle and lower or working (plus all the subdivisions, e.g. lower middle) took a while to evolve. At one point some people distinguished between the 'productive or useful classes' and the 'idle or privileged classes'. The term 'working class' was disliked by many because it implied that only those who belonged to such a class (typically manual labourers) actually worked. This gave rise to further distinctions; for example, the 'professional' and 'trading' classes, who did work, but not with their hands.

Warm-up

- Brainstorm students on what they associate with the word 'class' (see (i) above + first-class transport/degrees/hotels/food etc., i.e. a division according to grade or quality).

1   Social class and opportunity

- Students read the passage. As a whole class activity get students to hypothesise on the questions below. This, combined with the quetions on the student's page, could then lead on to a discussion on the USA, and students' opinions of the American dream.

   Questions: 1 What kind of book does the extract come from?   2 In which country was it set?   3 When was it written?   4 Who are the two speakers? (age, sex, position in life)   5 Is what speaker one says true?

🔑 1 *The Store Boy by Horatio Alger Jr, a 'rags-to-riches story'*
2 *USA*   3 *around 1900*   4 *Ben is a young man who has just saved this wealthy oldish woman from the hands of a pickpocket.*
5 *This is basically the American dream, which presumably a lot of people must have and still do believe in.*

- Students now look at the job list and rank the jobs according to the prestige value they associate with them and allocate them into a class (e.g. upper, middle, lower). Does their prestige ranking coincide with whether students would

actually like to do these jobs? You may need to change the list to suit your students.

(i) A survey in America ranked them in the following order: judge, physician (doctor), university professor, mayor of a large city, priest, novelist, police officer, carpenter, barber, truck (lorry) driver, restaurant cook, nightclub singer, taxi driver, garbage (rubbish) collector.

- Students then decide if there is a direct correlation between the prestige ranking, and possible rankings in terms of money, responsibility and job satisfaction. They then answer the questions.

Listening

- Students listen to an Indian student talking about the caste system in India. First brainstorm students on what they know about caste in India and then get them to answer these questions. (The tapescript is on page 18.)

   Questions: 1 Who are the untouchables and what did Gandhi call them? In what sense are they untouchable?
2 What kinds of things were untouchables not allowed to do?
3 Why didn't the British government do anything to help?

🔑 1 *Lowest caste, 'harijan' or 'children of god', considered to be spiritual polluters.*   2 *They couldn't use water wells, wear certain coloured clothes, go into temples, send children to certain schools.*
3 *They didn't want to risk revolt and thus become unable to exploit the country.*

Follow-up

- Students discuss what the Indian had to say about laws changing the way people think. The discussion could be extended to women's rights – do men still think it strange that women have the vote?

2   Classic and classical

- Tell students to look at the illustrations (or bring in your own), and choose the element they like best in each pair (modern or classical). They then explain their choices to the other members of the group. Discussion should move towards taste and changing fashions, tradition, etc.

(i) Students will probably ask you the difference between 'classic' and 'classical'. If you look at the examples in the complete *Oxford English Dictionary*, the two would appear to have identical meanings. In modern English 'classic' generally refers to the best of its kind, an acknowledged level of excellence (as in a classic film or football match, or indeed the Classics themselves), whereas 'classical' is often used in a more artistic context to refer to a particular historical (but not historic!) period. For definitions of these and other -ic/-ical words, see Swan, *Practical English Usage*.

Class

1 Social class and opportunity

'In this country, the fact that you are a poor boy will not stand in the way of your success. The most eminent men of the day, in all branches of business, and in all professions, were once poor boys. I dare say, looking at me, you don't suppose I ever knew anything of poverty.' 'No', said Ben.

barber
carpenter
garbage (rubbish) collector
judge
mayor of a large city
nightclub singer
novelist

physician (doctor)
police officer
priest
restaurant cook
taxi driver
truck (lorry) driver
university professor

1 In your country does a person's social position depend solely on merit and achievement (as it purports to in the USA)? Is there such a thing as a classless society? Would you like your society to be classless?

2 What social class are you in and what effect does this have on your life? Is it the same as your parents? Will it remain the same in the future?

3 Which kinds of people are the most respected and powerful? And who are the poorest, most rejected, unemployed or unemployable? Which class has the best life?

4 What rules of behaviour does each class/caste have in your country? How do people's goals and expectations vary from class to class (think about education, career, type and location of house)?

5 How much interaction is there between classes? How are inter-class and inter-racial friendships and marriages considered?

6 Would you prefer to belong to a cultural/social elite, or to be simply a member of the masses?

7 Is everyone born equal with equal opportunities? Should we all aspire to equality?

2 Classic and classical

Bach

3 Classroom

- The illustration shows various ways of arranging desks in a classroom. Students should examine the pros and cons of the various solutions, and then decide which is best for their needs. They should think in terms of desk size, shape and location; the position of the teacher and whiteboard; the constraints of their own particular classroom; and most importantly how all these factors affect teaching, learning, understanding and general communication (both teacher–student, and student–student). They also need to decide whether different subjects require different kinds of classrooms, ideal numbers in a class, etc.

Listening

- Students hear two teachers discussing which layouts they prefer. Students should identify which layouts are mentioned (some are mentioned twice) and whether the teachers approve or not, and why. One layout (3), mentioned by one of the teachers, is not drawn on the student's page. After listening once ask students to identify which one it is, then play the piece again and get them to draw how they imagine it is. They can then compare their drawings.

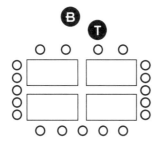

🔑 *1 a   2 c   3 see diagram   4 a   5 d*

📼 1 I think the two rows of desks could be good maybe in an exam situation where the teacher can control what's going on and make sure that nobody's cheating.

2 I really like the one where the teacher's part of a circle and they're not predominant, they're not dominating the lesson in any way, they're just one of the students and everybody can say their turn.

3 This is one that I thought would be good for project work, where you need a big work surface in the middle so pushing all the tables together, four tables all together to make one big square and the students all the way around the outside.

4 I really don't like this one with two rows of students some of them sitting behind the other, the ones in the back row wouldn't be interested in the lesson at all.

5 I think this one would be good for eh group discussions, small groups of people sitting round tables and the teacher sort of moving around, sometimes in the middle, and sometimes moving around the outside.

4 Classification

- Students decide their own criteria of judgement for classifying and comparing the categories (e.g. most useful/essential, important, efficient etc.). For each group they should do two rankings, both of which they should be able to justify. With talkative classes you may need to reduce the number of categories; in any case you may find students wandering off the main task of ranking and merely chatting about the subjects – it's up to you to decide whether this matters or not.

- Alternatively, tell students that there is one item in each class that does not fit with the others; their task is to spot the odd one out. There are no correct answers to this exercise.

Tapescript for **1 Social class and opportunity**

📼 A Could you tell me a little about the caste system in India? The only thing I've really heard about is the untouchables – perhaps you could start with them.

B Mahatma Gandhi called them 'harijan' or 'children of god', but most untouchables or 'Dalits' as they now call themselves, which means 'oppressed', consider this to be patronising and humiliating. The Dalits are, in any case, still literally untouchable in many rural areas of India.

A But where does this idea come from, in what sense are they 'untouchable'?

B Well, there is this divine ordering of society into castes, and anyone below a Shudra was considered to be untouchable. Basically they believe in Brahma which is an ultimate spirit of which there is a spark in all individuals, but divinities can only be approached if the human is pure. This means that there are certain polluting factors that have to be avoided, like people who deal with refuse and excretion, and these people were called the untouchables for that very reason.

A But that's terrible, you would have thought that the government would do something about it.

B Well your British government did little to help.

A What do you mean?

B Well, it was a well-known fact that people from a higher caste who found an untouchable on the road, would beat him down as they might destroy a rabid dog, and schoolchildren had to walk miles to go to school to avoid meeting a Brahman, and if by any chance they did see a Brahman they had to instantly make a howling noise, so as to warn him until they'd climbed up the nearest tree or whatever, and despite all this …

A This really is appalling. So why didn't the British try to stop it?

B They were too intent on preserving their Empire, because they knew that if they did anything radical, they might risk an uprising, and thus not be able to milk the country for all it was worth. This meant that the poor untouchables couldn't use the water wells, couldn't wear certain coloured clothes, couldn't go into temples, couldn't send their children to certain schools, in fact I remember my mother telling me of a woman in her village who'd been brutally assaulted and had her crop destroyed just because she'd sent her child to a public elementary school. Separate schools had to be opened.

3 Classroom

B = blackboard
T = teacher

a

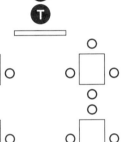

b

c

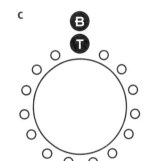

d

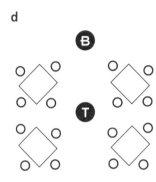

4 Classification

animals	cat, chicken, dog, horse	furniture	bed, chair, cupboard, table
century	first, fourteenth, sixteenth, twentieth	material	glass, gold, plastic, wood
clothes	jeans, shirt, tie, underwear	religion	Buddhism, Catholicism, Islam, Judaism
colour	black, blue, green, red	season	spring, summer, autumn, winter
country	Australia, N. Ireland, Japan, S. Africa	sport	baseball, football, golf, swimming
day	Monday, Friday, Saturday, Sunday	transport	bicycle, car, roller skates, tram
drug	aspirin, cigarettes, cocaine, love		
food	flour, milk, salt, sugar		

Difficulties

Warm-up

- Brainstorm students on what they consider to be difficult — don't be any more specific than that; just let the ideas flow, and write down the difficulties on the board. Then get them to copy the list and in groups rate the items according to difficulty.

1 Countries

- Students discuss which of the problems listed are currently or have been major difficulties for their country. Politically-minded students might like to discuss solutions to some of the problems.

Listening

- Students hear some people give their opinions on the difficulties of living in particular countries. Their task is simply to note down what these difficulties are.

1 *political uncertainty*   **2** *AIDS, gap between rich and poor*
3 *unemployment and racism*

1 The biggest problem, politically and socially speaking of China, is that it's not governed by laws but it's governed by people, and with the great political changes and instability in China, nobody can be sure of what is going to happen in the afternoon. So, it's a complete chaotic society.

2 The biggest problem in Uganda right now is the problem of Aids which is eh devastating the country a lot. There are lots of people dying and eh unfortunately nothing much can be done about it.

3 I think the most difficult thing in my country, in England, must be eh unemployment, it gets worse every year, and that's very hard to cope with. Also racism, despite all the different races that are there, racism's a big problem nowadays.

2 Brainteasers?

- Students look at the problems illustrated on their page and without actually beginning to solve them, try to estimate very quickly which looks the easiest to solve and which the most difficult (rating them **easy**, **quite hard** and **difficult**); students should also identify the type of problem it is (mathematical, general knowledge, etc.). Get feedback from the whole class.

- Now in groups, students have to resolve the problems. Give them a time limit, and see which group does the best. Then get feedback again to find out whether their estimations of difficulty coincided with reality.

1 *Suppose that the train for Manhattan left at 10.00, 10.10, 10.20 etc., and for Bronx at 10.01, 10.11, 10.21. This means that for the man to catch the Bronx train he must arrive just before 10.01; if he arrives after 10.01 but before 10.10 (i.e. a span of nine minutes as opposed to one) he will always catch the Manhattan train. Simple really!*

2 *This is part of a children's joke, which ends (i.e. after the question 'Do you give up?') with 'So did the donkey'. Most people tend to think that if you give them a problem to solve then there has to be a solution.*

3 *(a) man — as children we crawl on four feet, as adults two, as old people we may need a walking stick or two*
(b) in the dictionary
(c) a bald head

4 *children, data, mice (this like **5** cannot be reasoned over, either you know them or you don't).*

5 *9: Mercury, Venus, Earth, Mars, Jupiter, Saturn, Uranus, Neptune, Pluto. However, new planets are still being discovered: two in 1995/6.*

6 *207*

7

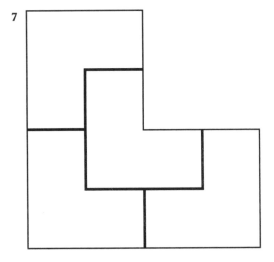

Difficulties

1 Countries

birth control	gap between rich and poor	inflation	political uncertainty	terrorism
border disputes	housing	national debt	pollution	unemployment
crime	illiteracy	natural disasters	racism	war
disease	immigration	political corruption	separatist movements	

2 Brainteasers?

1 A man who lives in New York has two friends, one who lives in the Bronx and one in Manhattan. He doesn't want to show any preference to one over the other, by visiting the first more than the second, so he devises a way in which the choice of person to visit is totally random. He decides always to use the train when he goes to see them, and to arrive at the station at a totally random time (he doesn't wear a watch). Trains for Manhattan and Bronx both leave from the same platform, and both at ten minute regular intervals so that there is one train to both places every ten minutes. So he decides that he will simply go to the platform and take the first train that arrives. However, he soon finds that nine times out of ten he goes to Manhattan, why?

2 There was a donkey alone on one side of the river and on the other there were some delicious carrots. The river was very wide and deep, so the donkey couldn't jump over it, and so long he couldn't walk round it. There was no bridge or boat and he couldn't fly and he couldn't swim. So how did he get across? How? Do you give up?

3 Answer just **one** of the following:

a What goes on four feet, then two feet, then three But the more feet it goes on the weaker it be?

b Where does Friday come before Thursday?

c What is it that no-one wishes to have, yet which no-one wishes to lose?

4 What are the plurals of these words: child, datum, mouse?

5 How many planets are there? Can you name them?

6 How many squares are there in this picture?

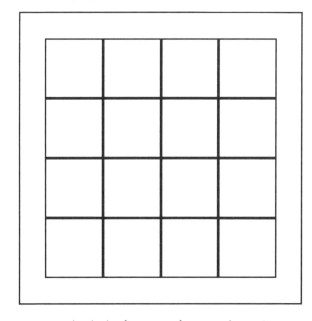

7 Can you divide this figure into four equal parts?

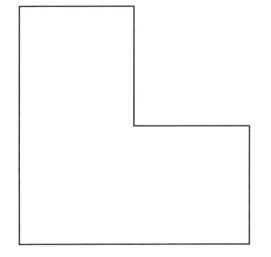

Difficulties

3 Projects

- Do the **warm-up** first. Then students imagine that they've been given the projects to do for their boss/teacher/leader or whoever. Their task is firstly to decide very quickly which would be the easiest project to do (in terms of skills and knowledge required). Get class feedback.
- Then in groups students should choose one or two projects, and do an in-depth analysis of what such work would entail. You might consider excluding projects 9–11, if you feel they might go against your students' values.
- Alternatively, or in addition, they could classify the projects according to which is the easiest, most difficult, most fun (or the one they'd most like to do), most time consuming, most dangerous, etc.
- In all cases, students should think of why these projects might have been conceived in the first place. Examples: **Project 3:** What is the current school leaving exam? How does this compare with exams in other countries? What are the problems with these exams? How could these problems be resolved? Do we really need a final exam anyway? **Project 10:** Why might they want to kidnap the child? What do they want to obtain? What would be the consequences for the child? How would students themselves feel about doing it?

Listening

- Students hear one person discussing which he would find the most difficult and why. With low level students simply tick off the ones he mentions and whether he thinks they are difficult or not. More advanced students should also list his reasons, where possible.

⚫ **7** *most difficult* **1** *difficult* **5** *difficult* **10** *easy* **9** *easy*

I'm convinced that the most difficult one of these is selecting the three most important books ever written. I mean it's a totally subjective decision and you're never going to arrive at some kind of unanimous decision on this one. It's also not very easy to make a very exact calculation between where you were born and New York. But I think perhaps you could do that. Finding the oldest man in the world, I suppose your first reference point would be the Guinness Book of Records but then they may not have got the right person. Kidnapping an important politician's child I think would be very easy; as would hijacking a plane, but neither of these are generally particularly successful afterwards.

4 Dilemmas

- First, ask students to insert appropriate verbs into the gaps; they can do this either individually or in groups. You can make it easier by writing the verbs on the board and getting students to insert them into the appropriate places.
- Get feedback and give students the answers.

⚫ **1** *learn* **2** *follow* **3** *be* **4** *obey* **5** *fake (show)* **6** *do* **7** *read* **8** *acquire or achieve* **9** *keep* **10** *accept*

- Now get them to choose the answers. In some cases they have to simply choose one of four possibilities (e.g. 1), other times they have to underline one of two possibilities (e.g. 4). They should then discuss the questions. In addition, they can also decide (where appropriate) which are the least (rather than the most) difficult. Some of these are a little heavy; you might need to be selective in the ones you ask your students to do. On the other hand, you might also like to add items.
- As class feedback, ask students which ones they had most difficulty in answering, either in terms of category or the elements within each category.

Difficulties

3 Projects

1 Calculate the exact distance between New York and your birthplace.

2 Design a house specifically for old people.

3 Devise a new form of examination for school leavers.

4 Dub an American film into your own language.

5 Find and interview the oldest man in the world.

6 Raise $100,000 for an extension to your school.

7 Select the three most important books ever written.

8 Write the script for the first episode of a soap opera.

9 Hijack a plane.

10 Kidnap an important politician's child.

11 Rob a million dollars from a bank.

4 Dilemmas

1 Which is the most difficult to ....?
   (a) to ride a bike
   (b) to swim
   (c) to drive
   (d) to use a computer

2 Which is the most difficult to ....?
   (a) an instruction manual
   (b) a recipe
   (c) a road map
   (d) your teacher's explanations

3 Who is it most difficult to ....?
   (a) a parent or a child
   (b) a teacher or a student
   (c) a woman or a man

4 Which are the most difficult to ....?
   (a) religious laws or state laws
   (b) your conscience or your desires
   (c) your parents or your teachers

5 Which is the most difficult to ....?
   (a) intelligence
   (b) interest
   (c) laughter
   (d) surprise
   (e) sympathy

6 Which is the most difficult to ....?
   (a) give or take
   (b) listen or talk
   (c) praise or criticise
   (d) speak in public or confide in private

7 Which is the most difficult to ....?
   (a) newspaper
   (b) novels
   (c) poetry
   (d) religious texts

8 Which is the most difficult to ....?
   (a) friendship or love
   (b) happiness or wealth
   (c) intelligence or beauty
   (d) a successful marriage or successful career

9 Which is the most difficult to ....?
   (a) a secret
   (b) a vow
   (c) one's health
   (d) youth
   (e) principles

10 Which is the most difficult to ....?
   (a) rejection in love
   (b) loss of all possessions through an earthquake
   (c) never having one's prayers answered
   (d) death of a close relative or friend

English

1 Old English

- Before handing out the photocopies, do the listening exercise.

Listening

- Students hear the first lines of an English poem – *The Battle of Maldon*. The poem begins mid-sentence – it is only a remnant. Offer a prize to whoever guesses what language it is.
  (There is no tapescript for this listening.)
- Now get students to look at the text (from the first history book written in English) and discuss the questions.

(i) Old English (OE) was considerably more complex than modern English and to modern eyes looks like a mixture of German and Latin. OE had the advantage of being much more phonetic (i.e. words were pronounced pretty much as they were written). Odd plurals in modern English (e.g. mouse – mice) are remnants from OE where many nouns had different singular and plural forms.

2 Spelling

- Write the following words on the board: bough, cough, enough, thorough, though. See if students know how to pronounce them. Ask them if they know why words that have a very similar spelling actually have a very different pronunciation.
- Now write the word 'ghoti' on the board and ask them how to pronounce it. Tell them it's pronounced 'fish' (*f* as in enou*gh* , *i* as in w*o*men, and *sh* as in na*ti*on). This word was actually invented by G. B. Shaw to prove how absurd English spelling is.
- Students now read the text, which is an explanation of why English spelling is so absurd.

(i) During the Second World War, Goebbels, the Nazi Minister of Propaganda, reputedly told his listeners that if they lost the war they would have to learn English – and English spelling, he said, is very, very difficult. Goebbels wasn't joking, apparently there are ten ways to spell the sound *ah* /ɑː/ as in father in English, 32 ways to spell *ee* /iː/ as in tree, 36 ways to spell /aɪ/ as in *eye*, and 17 ways to spell *sh* /ʃ/ as

in *sheep*. With regard to the computer study on English spelling, I conveniently forgot to mention in the passage that the 3% totally unpredictable words are also among the most frequently used in the language (e.g. answer, are, come, could, does, gone). The reason why 'c' and 's' are often pronounced the same (as in *nice* and *house*) is due to their alteration by analogy with French words like *grace* – Old English *is* and *mys* became *ice* and *mice*.

Latin too, has also had a considerable influence on English. When the Romans invaded England in 55 BC, they brought with them many military words, they even renamed some English towns, in fact all English towns that end in -chester, -cester etc. were originally Roman military bases from the Latin *castra* (meaning military camp, which is itself the plural of *castrum* meaning castle, fort or fortress). In 697 AD, St. Augustine went from Rome to Ireland and then to England to convert the heathens to Christianity, thus beginning the introduction of many Latin religious words. The monks, who were some of the very few who could write until the end of the Middle Ages, wrote of course in Latin. During the Renaissance many English scholars went to Italy to learn Latin. When they came back to their homeland they found the English language barbaric in comparison to Latin and they began altering some English spellings to make them look more like Latin, for example the Old English word for debt was *dette*, the *b*, which has always been silent, was introduced because it made the word look more like the original Latin *debitum*, and thus less vulgar. In more recent times, Latin (and Greek too) has been the root of many new scientific and technical words.

Confusion in English spelling is also due to a phenomenon called the 'Great Vowel Shift', in which although certain spellings had become fixed, the pronunciation changed – all the long vowels gradually came to be more pronounced with a greater elevation of the tongue and closing of the mouth. Scholars claim they can prove this by comparing the rhymes in poetry and determining whether the same words rhyme over the centuries.

Follow-up

- Give students a spelling test containing mistakes they typically make (e.g. ordinal numbers, Tuesday/Thursday, doubling, plurals and gerunds of words that end in 'y').

1   Old English

Breoton is gārsecges ēalond, ðæt wæs iūgeāra Albion hāten: is geseted betwyh norððæle and westdæle, Germanie and Gallie and Hispānie, þām mæstum dælum Eurōpe, myccle fæce ongegen. Þæt is norð ehta hund mīla lang, and tū hund mila brād. Hit hafað fram suððæle þā mægðe ongēan þe mon hāteð Gallia Belgica. Hit is welig, þis ēalond, on wæstmum and on trēowum misenlicra cynna, and hit is gescræpe on læswe scēapa and nēata, and on sumum stōwum

1 Do you think it would have been better if English had remained as it was 1000 years ago?

2 Can you read and understand your language of 1000 years ago? Is it important to be able to do so?

3 Has your language become simpler over the years?

4 Is your language phonetic, i.e. is it pronounced as it is written?

5 Are there many differences between your written and spoken language?

6 Do you think it is important to study your language, in terms of its origins and history, its literature and its grammar?

2   Spelling

Who says English spelling is difficult? A computer analysis of 17,000 English words has shown that 84% were spelt according to a regular pattern and that only 3% were so unpredictable that they would have to be learned totally by rote. Yet a professor at Cambridge University once declared that: 'I hold firmly to the belief ... that no-one can tell how to pronounce an English word unless he has at some time or other heard it.'

Believe it or not English spelling was at one time virtually phonetic: even the 'k' in 'know' was pronounced. At that time, the Old English period, words which now look as if they should rhyme (but don't), for instance, *bough, cough, enough, thorough* and *though*, actually all had a different spelling and it was therefore natural that they should be pronounced differently (boh, couhe, ɜenoɜ, þuruh, þeah).

It's really the French's (the Dutch's, too, but more about them later) fault that English spelling is so absurd, for in 1066 the Normans invaded England and brought with them their own language, Norman French. For the two centuries after this disastrous invasion poor old English was hardly ever written, because the language of the court, of law and of administration was French – the Normans held all the positions of power. About 40% of the words in the Oxford English Dictionary derive from French, the problem is that the English have always been hopeless at learning languages and they consequently mispronounced the majority of words which were introduced by the Normans into the English language. The Normans were also

responsible for the capital 'I' as in 'I am', and for introducing extra letters into existent words, such as the 'u' in tongue and guess.

The Dutch were also masters at introducing extra letters, but for economic not patriotic reasons. In 1465 printing was introduced into England, by a certain William Caxton, whose printing machines were manned by Dutch technicians. At that time printers were paid by the letter and as these technicians were a cunning bunch they knew that all they had to do to get more money was to make words longer; it is they in fact who are responsible for some of the 'oughs' which they added indiscriminately. They also had the excuse of not being able to understand English handwriting, so when in doubt they just added a few letters here and there. Until the 16th century line justification was achieved by abbreviating and contracting words, and also by adding extra letters (usually an 'e') to words, rather than extra space.

During the same period, with Latin and Greek becoming of renewed importance due to the Renaissance, many strange spellings were introduced because the people employed to copy the books became confused between English, French and Latin – there were no spelling rules or guides to help them. Then someone had the bright idea of producing a dictionary, yet this was little more than a list of 'hard words'. After all, it was reasoned, why should a dictionary include the words everyone already knew?

English

3 Fun with English

- This is a good exercise for the last lesson with an advanced group. Make it competitive by seeing which group manages to answer the most questions correctly. If you're short of time, only do the first part (questions **1–9**).
- In groups, students match the explanations (**1–9**) to the words, phrases and figures on their page. This should produce a lot of deduction language, as some questions initially seem to have more than one answer (e.g. 'radar' fits into two categories: acronym and a word that is spelt the same backwards and forwards); students may think that 'casanova' and 'saxophone' are composite words rather than being eponyms.

1 *noon*   **2** *close, lead, live, minute, row, tear, wind*   **3** *brunch, motel*   **4** *radar (radio detection and ranging), laser (light amplification by the stimulated emission of radiation)*   **5** *boycott, casanova, saxophone*   **6** *rhythm*   **7** *redivider (noon, radar)*   **8** *A man, a plan …; Was it a …;*   **9** *boot, party*

- Again in groups, they answer the other questions.

10 *It's a pangram, i.e. it's a sentence that contains every letter of the alphabet. People have invented shorter ones, but generally they're totally meaningless.*

11 *The top 25 are: the, of, and, to, a, in, that, I, it, was, is, he, for, you, on, with, as, be, had, but, they, at, his, have, not – nearly all these words derive from Old English. The most common letter is 'e', most common initial letter 't'.*

12 *I (the first person pronoun)*

13 *forty, although, Wednesday*

14 *bet, get and set all rhyme, are all infinitives (met isn't), and are all irregular (wet isn't, jet is a noun).*

15 *The* **Oxford English Dictionary** *has around 615,000 words, but scientific words would add a million or so more. We have about 200,000 words in common use (the result of so many invasions in the early history of the language). According to Bryson, German has about 184,000 words in common use, and French around 100,000. I know that the biggest Italian dictionary lists around 190,000 words. But, ask yourself, and your students: Does having more words imply that you can express yourself better? And does it mean that people whose languages have fewer words can't express themselves as well as us? I suppose it really depends on how many words you know and how well you use them.*

16 *According to an article in* **The Guardian** *at two years of age we have a vocabulary of 300 words, at five 5,000, at twelve most people reach their maximum of about 12,000 (the number as used by tabloids). Graduates: 23,000. But other experts believe we have around 15,000, about half the number Shakespeare used. A method outlined in Crystal for establishing words known estimated that a female office secretary in her 50s had a passive vocabulary of 38,300 and an active one of 31,500.*

17 *Give students some help before they give up. Tell them that James and John were doing a translation from Latin into English, and they had to translate the Latin equivalent of 'had had'. Anyway the answer is, if you haven't managed to work it out by yourself: James, where John had had 'had', had had 'had had'. 'Had had' had had the examiner's approval. Easy really! Did anyone win the prize?*

Writing

- Give students the following instructions. (a) Write a sentence that makes sense using all the letters of the alphabet – the shorter the better. (b) Write a short story (about 100 words) without using the letter 'a'.

Useful further reading: Baugh: *A history of the English language*; Bill Bryson: *Mother tongue*; Strang: *A history of English*; David Crystal: *The English language*.

3 Fun with English

WAS IT A CAR OR A CAT I SAW? ¿WAZ I TAƆ A ЯO ЯAƆ A TI ƧAW

close   row!   casanova   re|divider   minute t   NOON

win-d   boot   MOTEL

party   saxophone   live   RADAR   boycott

lead   te|ar   laser   BRUNCH

rhythm   A man a plan a canal –
Panama

1 A word which reads the same backwards, forwards and upside-down.

2 Seven words with the same spelling but a different meaning and different pronunciation (homograph, e.g. live /lɪv/ is a verb and /laɪv/ is an adjective, as in live concert).

3 Two words that consist of two words blended together, e.g. smog = smoke + fog.

4 Two acronyms, e.g. AIDS = acquired immune deficiency syndrome.

5 Three eponyms, e.g. sandwich was named after the Earl of Sandwich.

6 A word with no vowels.

7 A word which is spelt the same backwards as forwards.

8 Two sentences that read the same backwards and forwards (palindrome), e.g. Madam I'm Adam.

9 Two words, each of which can have several meanings, but whose spelling and pronunciation are the same (homonym).

10 What is strange about this sentence (think about the letters used)? The quick brown fox jumps over the lazy dog.

11 What do you think are the five most commonly used written words in English? And the most commonly used letter?

12 What word is the most commonly used in telephone conversations?

13 Which of the following words are spelt incorrectly? fourty, althought, misspelt, Wensday

14 What three things do three of these six words have in common? bet, get, jet, met, set, wet

15 How many words do you think there are in the English language?

16 How many words do you think the average English person knows?

17 Punctuate this sentence and win a free English course at your school!

In a Latin examination James where John had had had had had had had had had had the examiner's approval.

Fear

1 Phobias

- Before looking at the student's page, brainstorm students for a list of fears, theirs or other people's. These should include all kinds of fear from funfair attractions to snakes to open spaces. Write these on the board as they are called out. Students then copy the list and in groups discuss whether they suffer from any of them.

- Below is a list of common fears, some of which you might like to add to the students' list:

  AIDS, asking favours, bats, being a car passenger, being alone, being criticised/humiliated, being ignored, being in a strange place, being teased, being touched, being watched at work, blind people, blood, blushing, boredom, complaining about bad service, computers, crowds, dead animals, dead people, dentists, failing a test, fairground attractions (e.g. Big Dipper, etc.), God, growing old, high speeds, hospitals, hypodermic needles, impotence, job interviews, lifts, losing control, losing in love, losing parts of your body, making a fool of yourself, making speeches in public, mice, noise, not understanding jokes, people who seem insane, people with deformities, rape, snakes, suffocating, taking chances, taking exams, the dark, the opposite sex, the unknown, ugly people, using public lavatories, violence, water.

- Students should also discuss what problems their fears cause, whether their fears are totally irrational or not, how they manage to overcome them, and what physically and mentally happens to people when they're afraid.

- ⓘ 'I was so scared that my hair stood on end'. Why? When a cat's hair stands on end the cat looks bigger, so that with a bit of luck its enemy will be scared away. Other physical changes: your pupils dilate so that you can see better; your heart pumps your blood faster to give you more energy, and at the same time you become pale because the blood goes from your skin to the places it is needed – to the muscles, so that you can physically escape; and to the brain, so that you can think more clearly. You start to breathe faster because you need the oxygen. You stop digesting your food and you begin to sweat as this will evaporate and cool off your muscles.

- Alternatively, students look at the phobias in the first column on their page and decide which they think are the most common and whether they themselves suffer from them.

- ⓘ In the UK the order of commonness is: spiders, people and social situations, flying, open spaces, confined spaces, heights, cancer, thunderstorms, death, heart disease.

- Now get students to look at the second column. Tell them that these are all medically-established phobias. Ask them to discuss the consequences of having such phobias.

Writing

- Students write a short story about a person who had one or more of the phobias.

- ⓘ The word 'phobia' comes from Phobos, a Greek God who was called upon to frighten one's enemies. His likeness was painted on masks and shields for this purpose. The medical terms for some of these phobias are: *pogonophobia* (beards), *scopophobia* (being stared at), *gephyrophobia* (crossing bridges), *sitophobia* (food), *phasmophobia* (ghosts), *gamaphobia* (marriage), *eisoptrophobia* (mirrors), *neophobia* (newness), *triskaidekaphobia* (number thirteen), *hypegiaphobia* (responsibility).

2 Childhood fears

- Students read the text and discuss the questions in groups.

- ⓘ (1) The most common childhood fear is animals, beginning between the ages 2–4 and gone before age 10. The next most common is darkness, or rather what might be hiding in the darkness (ages 4–6). Other early fears: storms, thunder (and other loud noises), and lightning; being left alone for very long (until age 5). Fear of snakes, which affects about one third of children, is one of the few childhood fears which persists into adulthood. Little children don't have an innate fear of spiders, rats, and creepy crawlies (this is important to know for the experiment with Albert), yet for some unknown reason, by the time they're adults such fears may be very strong.

  (2) Other examples of conditioning: Pavlov's dog, religious sects, advertising, family pressures, subliminal messages, etc. The experiment with Albert took place in 1920, and for some reason, the psychologists did not have the opportunity to reverse the conditioning.

Writing

- Students choose one of the following as a composition title: (a) As a rule, what is out of sight disturbs men's minds more seriously than what they see. (b) Have you had any really terrifying experiences? Describe one. (c) Analyse why people like and dislike horror films.

3 Dirt

- Students read the text then cover it and try to remember (in groups or writing) all the strange things she does. They then re-read the text and finally discuss what life must be like for the woman's husband.

1 Phobias

cancer
confined spaces
death
flying
heart disease
heights
open spaces
people and social situations
spiders
thunderstorms

beards
being stared at
crossing bridges
food
ghosts
marriage
mirrors
newness
number 13
responsibility

2 Childhood fears

1 What were you afraid of as a child? Have any of these fears persisted into adulthood? Do you now have any rational fears (e.g. of not being able to pass tests and exams)?

2 Assuming such experiments as the one with Albert are useful, should individuals be 'sacrificed' for the progress of science/mankind?

3 Can you think of any other cases where conditioning is used? Can you resist conditioning?

To demonstrate how fears and phobias are acquired two psychologists deliberately established a rat phobia in a placid 11-month-old boy named Albert. When given a furry white rat to play with, Albert was initially delighted. However, like most children, Albert was afraid of loud noises. Whenever a steel bar behind Albert's head was struck with a hammer, Albert would jump and fall sideways onto the mattress he was sitting on. The noise was an unconditioned stimulus for the unconditioned response of fear.

Having established that Albert liked rats, the experimenters set about teaching him to fear them. Once again they offered him a rat, but this time, as Albert reached for it, one of the researchers struck a steel bar. Startled, Albert fell onto the mattress. The researchers repeated this procedure several times. Albert began to whimper and tremble. Finally, the rat was offered alone, without the noise. Albert fell over, cried, and crawled away as fast as his little legs could carry him. The rat had become a conditioned stimulus for fear. Further tests showed that Albert's fear generalized to other hairy or furry objects, including white rabbits, cotton wool, a Santa Claus mask, and the experimenter's hair.

3 Dirt

... one of the world's worst cases of fear of germs. In a fanatic pursuit of cleanliness a 49-year-old Australian housewife uses up more than 225 bars of soap on herself every month, wears rubber gloves even to switch on a light – and makes her husband sleep alone so that she won't be contaminated by him.

Every month, Mrs. X goes through 400 pairs of surgical gloves, 4,000 plastic bags – which she wears in multiple numbers over the gloves – and 360 rolls of paper towels.

She goes through dozens of boxes of laundry detergent every month because she washes her clothes six or seven times before wearing them. 'And I can't bear to walk on the floors outside my bedroom. I spread newspapers ahead of me as I walk through the house. But I can't stand leaving them lying on the floor – so I leave a room by walking backward and picking up the papers in my gloved hand. I'm terrified of encountering dirt. Whenever I feel particularly uneasy about dirt I wash my hands. Once I start I can't stop until I've used the entire bar. That usually takes about 90 minutes'.

Fear

4 Manias

- Students read the text and discuss the questions. Students might find this exercise a little repetitive if they have already done the Phobias exercise.

(*i*) (2) Other well-known manias: egomania, megalomania, nymphomania.

Listening

- Students hear a conversation, based on fact, about one woman's strange manias. Students answer the questions.

Questions: 1 Was the wife or the husband the first to be scared of going in lifts?   2 Name one of the rituals the wife went through before going to bed.   3 Did the husband know about these rituals before marrying her?   4 Did the therapist cure her?   5 What is the husband's problem and does his wife help him?

1 *wife*   **2** *slippers; lights on and off three times*   **3** *probably not*
4 *yes*   **5** *now dependent on his wife, who in turn ignores him*

A Gosh, did you see how that man was shaking in the lift? Sweat was just pouring off him.

B Yeah, I know. He's terrified of going in the lift without his wife.

A Without his wife. That's an odd one.

B Actually it's a really bizarre story, because she was the one who was originally scared of going in lifts on her own.

A She was?

B She must have had a traumatic upbringing or something but I know from a friend that it all began a few years ago when she started developing these strange manias. Like she had to walk upstairs with her eyes shut and if for some reason she had to open them while walking up, then she'd have to go back down and start again. Then before she went to bed she went through this ritual of having to put her slippers exactly in the mid point between the bed and the door, she even took a measuring tape with her when she went on holiday, so she could measure the distance out in hotels.

A You're joking?

B No, and then she goes through this routine of turning the lights on and off three times before she goes to bed. Then soon after she got married ...

A Did her future husband know about all this?

B I doubt it. Anyway soon after she got married she started to become dependent on her husband to do various things. And one of them was not being able to go in the lift without him. She just panicked without him. Anyway the husband eventually persuaded her to get help from a therapist who miraculously managed to cure her.

A Yeah, but I don't see how that explains why we've just seen him, the husband, like a nervous wreck in the lift.

B Oh right. Well probably the strangest thing in the whole of this story is that when his wife felt OK about going in lifts alone, or going shopping or whatever without him, he just couldn't cope.

A What do you mean?

B Well, just as she was totally dependent on him for doing virtually anything this apparently created a kind of co-dependence in him. So that when she no longer needed him, the justification almost for his existence as a separate entity disappeared, you know he thought he was indispensable and all that, with the result that now he can't do anything without her. The sad thing is that she's totally callous and virtually ignores him.

A That's terrible. But couldn't he just, you know, go to the therapist and get himself sorted out?

B You would have thought so, yeah.

5 The culture of fear

- Students may find this exercise sensitive.

- Students read the passage and discuss the questions.

Natal (South Africa). Students should be able to work this out from the names of the places, people and the black/white references. The piece was written in 1994 (i.e. during the big changes in South Africa).

Listening

- Students hear a father's fears for his young son. The task is simply to note down these fears.

loss of limbs, drugs, abuse, narrow-minded teachers.

I think you fear totally different things for your child than you do for yourself. I suppose the thing that worries me most, more than him dying almost, is that he might have some kind of accident and lose his arms or legs or something. When that kind of thing happens to you, I think you learn to accept it, when it happens to your child, you feel directly responsible, even if you weren't there at the time. I also worry that he might take drugs, get abused by some maniac; but even less dramatic things, like his teachers might try and curb his imagination and make him conform too much to their way of thinking.

4 Manias

Some people's insecurities manifest themselves in obsessive behaviours. A dipsomaniac, for example, has an abnormal and insatiable craving for alcohol. Those afflicted with kleptomania have a compulsive desire to steal things they don't actually need. More dangerous are pyromaniacs who feel compelled to start destructive fires. Other kinds of manias involve strange rituals to be performed when doing certain things. People who have developed rhythmmania, for example, give themselves a rhythm while doing something. This means that they will pace themselves to the door saying 'one two three, one two three' until they reach the door, then 'one two three' while they open it. This procedure is repeated for everything they do and if they get interrupted in the middle, i.e. before they've reached three, they have to go back and start again.

1 Analyse the implications of the four manias in the text, both for the people afflicted, their immediate family, and society in general.

2 Do you know of any other kinds of mania?

3 What would be the consequences of having any of the following manias?

anglomania (exaggerated liking for and imitation of English customs, manners, institutions), *callomania* (the delusion that one is beautiful), *chronomania* (perfectionism in time keeping), *metromania* (obsession for composing verse/poetry), *dromomania* (wandering), *hypomania* (being always on the go), *monomania* (excessive interest in one thing), *mythomania* (compulsively telling lies and believing them), *nostomania* (excessive nostalgia), *sophomania* (belief in one's own wisdom).

5 The culture of fear

Children suffer intolerably for the action and follies of their elders.
The horrors of the lives of some of the township children which Beverly Killian, senior lecturer in Psychology at Pietermaritzburg, has come across, can make one weep.
They live in a society which journalist Khaba Mkhize described as 'a community at war with itself. There have been so many deaths that most people have lost their sense of weeping.'
White children also have been brought up in a culture of fear, many taught that the world is unsafe and that they should not trust anyone.
'It is not only the political and criminal violence. Studies have shown that one in nine boys have been sexually abused, defined as any unwanted sexual attention by an adult. Domestic violence against children is not limited to any social group, occurring in the richest and poorest of households,' says Killian.
'The fear of today's children is primarily an interpersonal fear – a fear that some other person is going to harm them – which is a far more stressful than a fear, for example, of a nuclear war, the overwhelming fear expressed by the youth in Europe a decade ago,' says Killian.

1 What country do you think is being referred to in the article? What led you to this conclusion?

2 Do the fears mentioned reflect any of your own or your children's fears?

3 Who has the most to fear in your country?

4 What are the big fears of your generation? How do they differ from previous and future generations?

5 Which of the following figures do you fear: your parents, partner, teacher, classmates, priest, police, army?

6 On what occasion in your life have you been the most terrified?

Gender

ⓘ 'Gender' was originally used to classify nouns. Gender is now also used to distinguish between male and female behaviour: 'gender identity' (self awareness that one is either a male or a female), 'gender role' (the image that an individual presents to others based on culturally defined concepts of masculinity and femininity), 'gender specific' (of or limited to either males or females, e.g. eyes and hair colour are not gender specific), and 'gender gap' (the apparent disparity between men and women in values, attitudes, voting patterns, etc.).

Warm-up

- Before handing out photocopies or introducing the subject of gender, dictate these sentences: **1** A business executive discovers that a long-time employee has been stealing from the company. What should the executive do first? **2** A robber pulls a gun on a bank teller. What should the executive do first? **3** Someone witnesses a pedestrian being hit by a car. What should this person do first? **4** A relative is trying to give up smoking. What should the relative do first? **5** A nurse discovers a hospital patient has been given blood contaminated with the AIDS virus. What should the nurse do first?

- Students then try to 'image' or 'visualise' the situation and then write down one or two sentences to describe what the various people should do in the various situations. Don't let them ask any questions that might give the game away. The aim of this exercise is not immediately obvious. It is a test to see which pronoun students use when they describe the situation and what gender they see when they are imaging it. This exercise was invented by the author of a university paper on sexist language.

- Get some students to read out their sentences and ask them why they used 'she' for the 'nurse' and 'he' for the executive, and 'he' for the witness and member of the family (especially as in the last two cases we have no indication at all as to the sex of the person). Ask them if they think that the use of 'he' might be helping to perpetuate a male-dominated society, and whether they think it is important or not. Students will probably say 'no'.

1 Gender identity

- Ask students to read the text. Then do the listening. Finally, get students to invent their own related questions for them to discuss together (e.g. are men and women treated differently in your country, did your parents treat you differently from your brother/sister, would you do the same with your children, should differences between sexes be encouraged, etc.)

Listening

- Students hear three people (from China, Uganda and England) talking about how girls and boys and sisters and brothers are treated. There is no specific task, though what the speakers say should stimulate a discussion.

1 Boys can do many more things than girls can. And they, I mean, people expect from boys to become successful persons in their life and to provide for the family. Where the girls are supposed to end up getting married, bearing children and doing housework, and not having a career. So people are happy when they have a boy and they are not that happy when they have a girl.

2 In the past it, there used to be this difference because er ... the roles were different, like for a girl she would have to learn how to care for the house, to cook, and care for the children; and for a male, he had to learn how to dig and raise cattle, and do all kinds of heavy jobs that the woman wouldn't be able to do.

3 My parents always tried to treat me and my two younger brothers in exactly the same way, and they made a big point of saying that they were all treating us the same, but they did actually treat us differently, because I was a girl and they were boys.

2 Are you a woman or a man?

- The test is designed to be deliberately provocative. Students do the test individually and then compare their answers in groups. They should then redo the test, trying to decide which are the stereotypical female answers.

- Get class feedback, and find out which male students initially gave female answers, and vice versa. The conclusion should be that we all have both female and male characteristics.

3 Female facts

- Students discuss the facts.

Listening

- Students hear the answers to the facts about women. Students note down if they were true or false, plus any other information they hear. (The tapescript is on p. 34.)

↝ *1T 2T 3T? 4F 5T 6 not mentioned*
also mentioned: women float better; twice as many women diet; 44% of women in Britain work part-time, and only 6% of men; women hate lack of communication and untidiness.

Gender

1 Gender identity

A small girl learns, by the time she is two or three, that she is a girl. Her books tell her with big pictures and little words what girls like and what course she is bound to follow. Girls can become mommies, nurses, or teachers. The books do not show sisters leading brothers. They do not show girls making discoveries, creating inventions, making important decisions; boys do these things! Girls learn early that what boys do is better.

Children get spoken and unspoken messages from their parents that communicate the relative value of blue and pink. Parents have very different ideas about what is appropriate behaviour for girls and boys. Their expectations influence how they treat their children and have a snowball effect on the small differences between children when they are born.

ILLUSTRATED
CHILDREN'S STORY
BOOK

2 Are you a woman or a man?

1 **If your car breaks down do you ... ?**
(a) open the bonnet and have look inside (b) flag someone down

2 **A man and a woman go to the restaurant. Who pays?**
(a) the man (b) the woman

3 **What would your ideal house be?**
(a) easy to clean (b) big and impressive

4 **On holiday where do you keep the money?**
(a) in your back pocket (b) in a bag tied round your neck

5 **What is your motto?**
(a) If you don't take risks you don't get anywhere. (b) Better the devil you know than the devil you don't.

6 **Are your friends ... ?**
(a) more intelligent than you (b) better-looking than you

7 **Do you understand people better who communicate using ... ?**
(a) body language (b) the written word

8 **What animal frightens you the most?**
(a) a mouse (b) a shark

9 **In a war would you ... ?**
(a) fight for your country (b) leave for a neutral country

10 **Which do you prefer reading?**
(a) books (b) magazines

Score A typical man would say that the woman's answers would be: 1b, 2a, 3a, 4b, 5b, 6b, 7a, 8a, 9b, 10b. A typical woman might think otherwise!

3 Female facts

1 Women live longer than men.

2 Women hear better than men.

3 Women communicate better than men.

4 Women need men more than men need women.

5 Women get married younger than men do.

6 Women are more intelligent than men.

Tapescript for 3 Female facts

Here we go then, some totally useless and not so useless information about women. Women live longer than men, well we all knew that didn't we? But did you know that women are four times as likely as men to live to a hundred? Women have slightly better hearing than men. Pardon? Ooh, here's an odd one – women float better than men, but why would anyone want to do a study on floating, I don't know. Anyway here's the next one, twice as many women diet as men, actually I would have thought it would have been more than that, well there you go. Forty four per cent of women in Britain work part-time. And the men? Only six per cent. Well, that figures I suppose. Women only get half as much in their pension as men do. In a survey of what women hate most in their men, they said: lack of communication, no kidding, with untidiness running second. Wonder if they did a similar survey with men. Ooh, look at this, a woman's pulse rate doesn't rise as high as a man's does when kissing – I wonder why? Ah! And here's the result of survey on males, yes, it's true ladies, men need women more than women need men. A survey of thirty thousand people revealed that men are much more bored, disorganised and lonely without a mate than women are. Well, that I have to admit, I'd always suspected. Women get married younger than men do – well I knew that, but I must say I wonder why we get married at all after reading all these statistics.

4 HIStory, HERstory, or HYSteria?

- Make sure you've done the warm-up. Before students read the text, tell them to write down as many words as they can connected to gender-linked jobs (e.g. actor/actress, fireman/firewoman) and gender-linked relationships (e.g. wife/husband). Then discuss if and when and how these should be made gender-neutral (e.g. firefighter).
- Students read the text and answer the questions in groups.

🔑 *Possible solutions to question 5*
(a) We will ... No one ... (b) Our origins; the origin of the human species ... (c) Shall I let them in? Shall I let whoever it is in? (d) All students must have their own books. (e) Our neighbours are ... (f) ... their head ... (g) The English are very reserved. (h) An English person's home is their castle (sounds awful now, but in a 100 years or so people won't think twice about it). (i) Ask the average person and they would say ... (j) Users can use their mouse to move the cursor.

ⓘ The use of *they* and *their* with a singular subject is frowned upon by purists, but is becoming increasingly common and serves a very useful purpose. But there are circumstances where it is impossible to avoid he/she situations, and feminists have answered this by coming up with new gender neutral pronouns.

Extra

- To test whether students have got the message of this unit, tell them this very famous story: A father and his son were involved in a tragic car accident, the father was killed. His son was taken to hospital and when he was wheeled into the operating theatre the doctor exclaimed: 'Oh no, that's my son!' Why did the doctor say this?

🔑 *The doctor, of course, was the boy's mother!*

4   HIStory, HERstory, or HYSteria?

Many feminists have tried to rid the English language of words containing the word 'man' or any word which indicates the gender of the person it refers to. For example:

woman/women → womyn/wimmin   fireman → firefighter
craftsman → artisan   waiter/waitress → waitron
history → herstory

'Neighbour' and 'survivors' (*below*), which should be neutral terms for both sexes, here obviously only refer to men, women being excluded as second class citizens.

Maniac kills neighbour and wife

Plane crash: 30 survivors
including 10 women

Here are some words that people have invented to avoid the generic 'he' problem; only the first is ever really used:

s/he, xe, tey = he or she   per = person = he or she

peep = singular of 'people'   herm, wm = her or him

Literature and television are often blamed for the tendency towards male protagonism. Nearly 80% of the action in books (particularly children's books) and TV programmes is carried out by boys and men, so that female readers/viewers, consciously or not, see themselves in a subservient role.

In 1984 the federal government of Australia decided to expunge all sexist words from the statute books – an incredible 50,000 offending words were found.

1 Feminist scholars maintain that the generic 'he' and similar words 'not only reflect a history of male domination' but also 'actively encourage its perpetuation'. How do you think this is possible?

2 Does your language have a generic pronoun which is neither masculine or feminine, and which can refer to the two sexes indiscriminately? If you don't have one, how do women feel about having to use 'he' to describe a generic person? If nobody cares about it in your country, why is it that people care so much about it (almost to the point of obsession) in English-speaking countries?

3 Feminists coined the word 'Ms.' as an exact equivalent to Mr. Why do you think 'Ms.' was invented? Do you think it was needed? If you are a woman, why would(n't) you use this word?

4 Male words have tended to retain their connotations of power and independence, whereas female ones have become associated with triviality, dependence and sex. Compare, for example, bachelor/spinster, governor/governess, master/mistress. Do the same kind of distinctions exist in your language? Now do you agree that even one's language can contribute to the way we see the world, i.e. a male dominated world? You don't? Sigh!

5 How could you convert the following sentences into 'gender neutral' sentences?

a   Man will never conquer space.

b   Man's origins are still not fully understood.

c   Someone is at the door. Shall I let him in?

d   Each student must have his own book.

e   My neighbour and his wife are on holiday.

f   Anyone who thinks that needs his head seeing to.

g   Englishmen are very reserved.

h   An Englishman's home is his castle.

i   Ask the man in the street, he would probably tell you that …

j   The user can use his mouse to move the cursor.

Home

The original meaning of the word 'home', in English and many other Indo-European languages too, was of a safe dwelling place, a village, even a world. In Old English it came to mean a fixed abode where people habitually lived and sometimes was extended to include members of a family (home circle). Webster's says that 'house' (from a reconstructed Indo-European base meaning) comes from the same root as 'sky' and was used to mean a 'covering and concealing'. Our modern usage of these two words can be traced back to these original meanings. 'Home' has connotations of a feeling of belonging, a centre of affection, a place where you can find refuge and rest, it is something intimate and private. If you think about the words 'homely' and 'homemaker' (as opposed to 'housekeeper'), you immediately get the feeling of an atmosphere, a family (in fact we talk of a 'broken home' where the parents are separated). It even has the sense of a destination – 'homeward bound' (old hippies will remember the Simon and Garfunkel song), and also a nation (home vs. foreign policy; Browning's poem *Home thoughts from abroad*). Generally, 'home' only refers to one's own place; we'd say 'I went round to Adrian's house' not his 'home'. House, in the meaning of a covering or storage place, is clear in such things as a greenhouse, henhouse, the House of Commons, a clearing house, etc. It is a physical structure not a place where one should supposedly receive kind treatment and feel relaxed ('Make yourself at home.').

Ever wondered why we say to go/arrive/get home (i.e. without any preposition)? This is a remnant from Old English where the accusative case was used without a preposition, like the Latin 'domum', with the sense of 'to one's house, to home'.

Warm-up

- Brainstorm students on the difference between 'house' and 'home'. Then get them to think of all the compound words beginning with 'home' (e.g. homebred, -coming, -land, -less, -made, -maker, -stead, -stretch, -video, -work) and compare these with any expressions they can think of containing 'house'. This should confirm and consolidate the difference between home and house. Then go on to **Homesick?**

1   Home sweet home

- Do the listening exercise before students look at their page.

Listening

- Students hear two people talking about typical houses in their country. Students then look at their page. With low-level classes, after listening, students should identify which kind of house was being talked about (**picture d**); higher-level classes should also note the minor differences between the two descriptions.

1 Well in South Africa there are many more blacks than whites, and a lot of the blacks, most of them I think live in rural areas, and they have round houses with thatched roofs, and em mud walls, and em no chimneys, and there's a gap between the wall and the roof for ventilation.

2 In Uganda we live in a thatched house, that is the roof is made with sticks and grass, the wall is made of, of mud, covered, of sticks covered with the mud wall, the floor is also smeared with mud to make it smooth; and between the roof and the wall there is a space of about half a metre for ventilation. There are two windows usually on the sides.

- After the listening, students discuss the other illustrations. In groups they decide in which countries such houses would be typically found.
- Students now discuss why they were built in such a way (and with what materials), and what the advantages and disadvantages are of such houses (in terms of living conditions, cost, maintenance, appearance, etc.).

Follow-up

- Students discuss the housing situation in their country – where is the best place to live (both on a national, regional and city level), whether it's easy to rent or buy.

2   Homesick?

- Students read the passage and as a whole class discuss questions 1 and 2.

The passage comes from a boy's story, *Tom Sawyer*, by Mark Twain, a very famous American novelist. In this particular extract Tom and his friends have gone camping.

- Students now discuss the other questions and then do the listening exercise.

Listening

- Students hear what three people (from Uganda, South Africa and China) miss most when they are away from home. They should fill in a table like the one below.

	miss	*don't miss*
1	culture, family	not mentioned
2	family, friends, nature	racism
3	culture, festivals	censorship, sexism, class

1 What I miss most is about Uganda is er the culture I grew up in, the people I grew together with. I miss a lot my family because I don't get to see them very often.

2 I miss family and friends but I also miss the beautiful beaches and the mountains and the lovely countryside. I don't miss the racism although it is a very different place since the elections in 1994.

3 I don't miss the lack of freedom. I don't miss the difference between men and women, I don't miss the class differences, censorship, things like that, but I do miss all the traditional cultural part, even food, festivals, the atmosphere.

1 Home sweet home

2 Homesick?

They found plenty of things to be delighted with, but nothing to be astonished at. They discovered that the island was about three miles long and a quarter of a mile wide, and that the shore it lay closest to was only separated from it by a narrow channel hardly two hundred yards wide. They took a swim about every hour, so it was close upon the middle of the afternoon when they got back to camp. They were too hungry to stop to fish, but they fared sumptuously upon cold ham, and then threw themselves down in the shade to talk. But the talk soon began to drag, and then died. The stillness, the solemnity that brooded in the woods, and the sense of loneliness, began to tell upon the spirits of the boys. They fell to thinking. A sort of undefined longing crept upon them. This took dim shape, presently — it was budding homesickness. But they were all ashamed of their weakness, and none was brave enough to speak his thought.

1 Who are 'they'? Where are they?

2 How are they feeling? Why are they ashamed of the way they are feeling?

3 Have you ever been camping with some friends? Have you ever been exploring?

4 When was the first time you slept away from home? How did you feel? What home comforts did you miss the most?

5 When you go to another place or abroad, what do you miss the most about your home town and country? (family, friends, pets, house, food and drink, culture, sense of humour, TV, shops, institutions, not being able to speak your native language?)

6 How often do you phone and write home when you are away?

Home

3 Homeless and homeland

This could be a very touchy subject for a lot of people. Test the ground before embarking on it.

- Students look at the picture of the refugee camp and imagine how life must be for such people. They should then answer the questions.

Writing
- 'Charity begins at home'. Discuss.

4 Home, language and nation

This could be a very touchy subject for a lot of people. Test the ground before embarking on it.

(i) Language has not always been a unifying element in Europe either (e.g. Ireland and the former Yugoslavia), but it has been in separatist groups in Spain and France. Language is, in any case, certainly something people feel very strongly about – the Flemish used to object to their children being taught French in French.
- Students read the passage and discuss the questions.

3 Homeless and homeland

1 Is your country currently home to any refugees? How well has your country accepted them?

2 What kinds of conditions do refugees live in? What problems do they face? Imagine a typical day in the life of a refugee.

3 Leaving aside refugees, and concentrating on general immigration, imagine you are members of a government department which decides who to give permanent visas to. Put the following in order of preference:

English teachers

married sons and daughters of citizens of your country

people escaping from a war

people seeking political asylum from countries that are not at war

people who are prepared to do very humble jobs (e.g. cleaning, refuse collection) at a cheap price

people with an internationally recognised extraordinary ability in (four separate categories): science, art, business, athletics

spouses and unmarried children of lawfully permanent residents (i.e. people who were not born in your country, but who can legally live there indefinitely)

unmarried sons and daughters of citizens of your country

The number of refugees in the world varies from year to year, and figures can never be very accurate. In the early 1990s, for example, nearly 7,000,000 Afghans had already left or were leaving their homeland, and another two and a half million Palestinians had no fixed home. In many African countries people were on the move (Mozambique, Eritrea, Somalia, Liberia, Angola, Rwanda, Sudan etc.) and in the Far East as well (Cambodia, Vietnam and China). In this period too, we saw the beginnings of the problems in what used to be Yugoslavia.

The countries which accommodate refugees tend to be neighbouring countries (e.g. Thailand accepted half a million people escaping from Myanmar, Laos and Cambodia, Pakistan 3.5 million from Afghanistan, and Iran 3.0 million from Afghanistan and Iraq). Other countries, such as the United States, accept people from a variety of countries and have strict laws on who can and cannot be accepted.

4 Home, language and nation

Most people tend to feel at home where people speak the same language as they do. In fact, boundary disputes at the end of the two World Wars were generally based on linguistic groups, and this was reflected in the subsequent transfers of populations. Dictators, such as Mussolini and Hitler, exploited this principle when they tried to introduce speakers of their languages into areas which they claimed belonged to them. So Mussolini urged Italians to migrate to the South Tyrol, and Hitler called on German-speaking people in Austria, Poland and Alsace to unite. However, in many parts of the world, there are communities which are defined by the religion they share, rather than the language they speak.

1 How long has your nation existed with its present borders? Are these fair borders?

2 Does everyone feel at home in your country or are there some who would prefer either some kind of home rule (i.e. local self government) or to become a separate state? Do you personally feel you belong to your country?

3 What do you think binds people together most — language, religion or something else?

4 Did your country ever colonise other countries? When and why? Are these countries still colonised? What rights do their residents have in your country? Was your language ever adopted there?

5 Was your country ever colonised by another country? How do you feel about this? What were the advantages and disadvantages of such a situation?

Intelligence

Warm-up

- In groups, ask students to define intelligence.

ⓘ Here are some psychological definitions: the ability to adjust to the environment and to new situations; the ability to learn or the capacity for education; ability to employ abstract concepts and to use a wide range of symbols and concepts; ability to solve problems; verbal facility. But your students should come up with some more down-to-earth definitions. One American researcher, J. P. Guilford proposed no fewer than 120 separate kinds of 'intelligence', grouped under main general headings like memory, reasoning, and divergent and convergent thinking.

1 A born genius?

- Get students to read the extract and then immediately proceed to the listening exercise before they answer the questions.

ⓘ (3) Is the fact that Shakespeare was born in England and not Siberia relevant? (5) Experiments have proved that the more intelligent a dog is the less likely it is to crack up under pressure. Similarly, war experience has shown that intelligent soldiers are less prone to shell shock and other psychological pressures than their less intelligent companions.
The photo shows Ganesh Sittampalam who got a first-class degree in Mathematics at the age of 13.

Listening

- Students hear three possible versions for the final paragraph of the reading extract. They have to decide which was the original one, and whether the other two contain reasonable ideas or not. Students then discuss the questions.

Key: 1

1 It's a mistake for parents to think their child is a genius. Let time decide that. But it is an even greater mistake for parents to think their child has no talent at all. The geniuses of history are telling us how much higher we could reach if only we believed in ourselves.

2 Parents should thus waste no time in finding out whether their child has hidden talents or not. If they do not do so, the world may be deprived of someone, who, given the chance, might have been able to find a cure for cancer, a solution to the world's energy problems, or simply a way to bring warring nations to their senses.

3 Don't listen, then, to those who would foist piano lessons on children who have barely begun to talk, or cryptic crosswords on kids who've only just begun to read, or mind-bending mathematical problems on youngsters who have only just learned to reason. Think above all about your child's happiness and ask yourself whether a child who studies the violin six hours a day is more content than one who spends the same time with their friends and toys.

2 A head start

- Students read the text and discuss questions in groups.

ⓘ (5) Parents who were motivated enough to use the devices have probably done a lot of stimulating of their child after its birth as well.

Intelligence

1 A born genius?

1 Are people born intelligent or do they acquire intelligence?

2 Is talk of genius elitist? Are not all children equally important?

3 How much effect does someone's environment bear on their intelligence?

4 Is it possible to distinguish intelligence from imagination, creativity and common sense?

5 Is a person's happiness and ability to adapt in any way related to how intelligent they are?

Ganesh Sittampalam

When a 13-year-old boy obtains a first class degree in mathematics or an 8-year-old plays chess like a future grand master, they are hailed as geniuses. Whether they really are geniuses or just precocious talents, their achievements raise fascinating questions.

Where does the quality of genius come from? Is it all in the genes or can any child be turned into a genius? And if parents do have a potential genius in the family, what should they do?

One thing is certain: it is difficult for parents to get it right. If I had been Mozart's headmaster I would have told his father – a typical over-ambitious parent – to stop pushing his son so hard at his music and let

WHEN DO GENIUSES REACH THEIR PEAK?

YEARS
50
40
30
20
10

| SHAKESPEARE 1564–1616 | MOZART 1756–1791 | EINSTEIN 1879–1955 | PROF. STEPHEN HAWKINGS Born 1942, still going |

| NEWTON 1643–1727 | BEETHOVEN 1770–1827 | SIR ISAIAH BERLIN Born 1909, still going | |

Wolfgang Amadeus enjoy being a boy rather than a prodigy.

True genius is inherited in the genes and to turn a home into a private intellectual hothouse reminds me of factory farming. The danger is that it may be done for the glory of the parent rather than the good of the child.

Another problem is that outstanding genius does not always reveal itself at a young age. While Mozart played the piano blindfold as a child, Shakespeare did not make much impression on his teacher. Nor did Charles Darwin, because the future scientific genius was bored by his narrow classical curriculum.

2 A head start

Sometimes new parents can't wait to give their children a head start in life. They begin before the baby is even born. In hopes that sounds will somehow influence the fetus in their womb, zealous moms-to-be have attended classical concerts or kept tunes playing constantly at home. Now there is an updated, high-tech version of that technique: a contraption that delivers complex sonic patterns to unborn children, to excite the fetal nervous system and exercise the baby's brain.

'This is not a yuppie toy,' says its inventor. 'We have barely literate families who are using the tapes.' To date, 1,200 children – the oldest of whom is now four – have 'listened' to the recordings. Last year 50 of the youngsters, ranging in age from six months to 34 months, were given standardised language, social and motor-skills tests. Their overall score was 25% above the U.S. norm.

1 If you were pregnant would you use a sonic-stimulation device?

2 Why do parents want to give their children a head start? Is it really necessary?

3 Are there any dangers in over-stimulating children?

4 Are super-intelligent children necessarily any happier than their 'normal' friends?

5 Can you see any holes in the interpretation of the tests mentioned at the end of the text?

6 In what ways should parents stimulate their children?

Intelligence

3 Intelligence test

- The intelligence test is best done in groups. Make it competitive by giving a 15-minute time limit and see which group has got the most correct answers.

(i) The first serious intelligence tests were conducted in 1905 by Alfred Binet. They were done at the request of the French government who wanted to identify children with learning disabilities so that they could be given extra tuition. In 1916 Binet's tests were adapted by an American psychologist from Stanford University. IQ, or 'intelligence quotient', tests had begun. The questions mainly related to numbers, words and objects. The average IQ is 100. Research has shown that cultural background, motivation (or lack of it), class differences, changes in family structure and home conditions, even the relationship between the tester and the person being tested, all affect the final IQ score achieved. Binet was convinced that a person's intelligence changes during their lifetime, but others believe it is inherited and doesn't vary.

⚷ *Here are some answers. If your students come up with other answers make sure they can justify them*

1 *(a) You are more likely to do one activity, than that same activity plus another one. People who base their answer on Katie's interest in animal rights are ignoring the mathematics of the problem (i.e. probabilities).*

2 *O. They are the first letters of the numbers one to twenty (One, Two, Three).*

3 *The probability is zero. If nine people have their own hats, then the tenth must too.*

4 *They are Siamese twins.*

5 *They depend on the position of the letter 'h': hospital, those, ethics, eight, teach, enough.*

6 *(a) Aunt. The only female. (b) y (the others are in alphabetical order) (c) woman: wife (the others are family relations).*

7 *Do exercises like this really prove anything? These kinds of tests don't necessarily demonstrate intelligence.*

8 *(a) Not necessarily, it may go in one ear and out the other. The news only informs us about what journalists think we might find interesting. (b) Studying hard doesn't necessarily mean good results, the opposite is also true. (c) She might just be playing games. (d) They could equally be brothers, or brother and sister. (e) He wasn't an orphan before he murdered his parents. (f) Biographical is more likely. (g) Unless her daughter was adopted, this sentence is nonsense. (h) How can you see an iceberg if it's already melted?*

9 *None, an unlisted number doesn't appear in a phone book.*

10 *Yes, freeze the water in the two cans before putting it into the empty container.*

Writing

- Students write the answers to question 8. This involves using conditionals and modals for deduction.

Useful further reading:
A. Gellatly: *The skilful mind*; J. F. Fixx: *Solve it.*

3 Intelligence test

1 **Katie** is 30 years old, single, with a lively personality. At university she studied languages and was also involved in an animal protection group. She loves travelling. Which of the following two statements is more probable?

a) *She teaches English as a foreign language.*

b) *She teaches English as a foreign language and is a member of the Worldwide Fund for Nature.*

2 **WHAT IS** the first letter of the following sequence (it is not 'E')?

```
? T T F F
S S E N T
E T T F F
S S E N T
```

3 **TEN** people, all wearing hats, were walking along a street when a sudden wind blew their hats off. A helpful boy retrieved them and, without asking which hat belonged to which person, handed each person a hat. What is the probability that exactly nine of the people received their own hats.

4 **T**wo women and a man are sitting at a table arguing. Suddenly one of the women pulls out a gun and shoots the man. The case goes to court, and the first woman is found guilty. However, the other woman, who the judge knows is innocent, has to go to prison as well. Why?

5 **T**HESE words have been put in order – following what rule?

hospital, those, ethics, eight, teach, enough

6 **WHICH IS** the odd one out?

a) actor, aunt, bachelor, king, nephew

b) y, m, s, u, x

c) aunt: uncle, woman: wife, father: son, brother: sister.

7 **Divide** up the words as fast as possible.

DoeXErciSESLiketHISreaLLyprOVEANytHIng?

TheSEKINdSOftestsDOn'tnECESSarilydemONstraTEINTelligenCe.

8 **EXPLAIN** why the following sentences are not necessarily logical.

a) *Charles is very well informed – he watches the news every night.*

b) *Julie doesn't study, so she won't pass the exam.*

c) *Jodie is a 10-year-old who spends most of her time on the computer. She must be intelligent.*

d) *Devan and Taman are both secretaries. They have the same mother and were born on the same day at the same time. Therefore they must be twin-sisters.*

e) *He murdered his parents and then pleaded for mercy because he was an orphan.*

f) *She's still writing books. Autobiographical mainly.*

g) *She hasn't had any children and she's going to make sure her daughter doesn't either.*

h) *We saw an iceberg that had completely melted.*

9 **13%** of the people in a certain town have unlisted phone numbers. You select 300 names at random from the phone book. What is the expected number of people who will have unlisted numbers?

10 **YOU** have two cans filled with water and a large empty container with no internal divisions. Is there a way to put all the water into the large container so that you can tell which water came from which can?

Justice

Warm-up

- Students discuss qualities of an ideal judge.

(i) The spirit of justice was female in classical paganism, are women therefore innately better at judging than men? How has our sense of justice changed over the centuries? Does one's own sense of justice change much during one's life?

1 Juries

- Brainstorm students on what kind of people should and should not be able to serve on a jury, and should be allowed to be excused. Should jury work be compulsory? Should compensation be given for loss of time and money? Then do the listening.

Listening

- Students hear about the origins of the jury system in England. After listening twice, choose a few students and ask them the following questions.

Questions: **1** In what way were the original juries different from today's? **2** How do you qualify for jury service? **3** Who is exempt?

Back in the middle ages, a jury was a group of neighbours who were asked questions under oath by one of the king's men to find out what rights the king had in that area. For example, they might have to name all the landowners of their district and say how much land each of them had; or name all the persons in their district who they suspected of murder, robbery or other crimes. The job of these people, usually twelve, was not to pass any judgement but simply to declare the truth. This system gradually evolved into a group of twelve people who had to give a verdict in court on an accused person or people. Until 1974 in England jurors had to be house-owners and the age was restricted, which basically meant that they were male, middle-aged and middle class, with all the ideas that belong to such a group. Now to qualify you have to be on the electoral list, no older than 65, and a UK resident. Various people are ineligible for jury service such as members of the legal profession, police officers, ministers of religion, the mentally ill, and anyone who

has served a prison sentence in the last 10 years. Members of Parliament, members of the armed forces, and doctors can be excused from jury service. Because of the length of some trials, jurors are paid travelling and subsistence allowances, along with some compensation for loss of earnings.

- Finally in groups students imagine that they are members of a jury whose task is to consider the five cases (on the student's page). Before beginning the trial students need to decide together what options are available as sentences (from acquittal to life imprisonment). Students also need to take into account the circumstances.
- Alternatively, students could think of non-prison punishments to fit the crime.

(i) (1) Would it change things if the woman had shot the man dead, or paralysed him for life? What is legitimate defence? (2) Would it make any difference if the lights had been on green? If the man's wife had not been pregnant? What if it had been an ambulance that had killed someone going through on red? What if the people killed were deaf/blind? In any case hasn't the man paid enough just by what he will have on his conscience – maybe just taking away his driving licence would be enough. (3) Discuss whether it should be 'finders keepers' when discovering ancient artefacts, whether such things belong to the person on whose land they were found, or whether they are part of the national heritage. (4) In May 1993 Lee Jang Rim was sentenced to one year in prison for predicting that the world would end on 28 October 1992. Tell students Rim's sentence after they have had their discussion. Consider why the judge sentenced him for one year only. Was Rim directly responsible for the suicides? Do we need to protect people from their own gullibility? (5) The company in question, initially explained that they didn't have the $32 billion needed to pay all claimants, so merely offered losers their apologies. Then, after death threats to employees, riots and stonings, they paid out $20 in 'goodwill prizes'.

2 Punishing children

- Students read text and discuss questions in groups.

1 Juries

1 This woman shot in the knee the unarmed man who had broken into her house. He later spent six months in hospital as the result of his injury and is still unable to walk.

2 This man drove through traffic lights on red and killed two people. He was taking his pregnant wife to hospital, she actually delivered the baby whilst still in the car.

3 This man is a private art collector who received items stolen by grave robbers who had been stealing from 3000-year-old tombs at an archaeological site. The robbers are also in court for having destroyed many pottery artefacts during their raid.

4 This preacher predicted that the world was going to end in three months. He accepted millions of dollars in donations from believers who had sold their homes, abandoned their families and quit their jobs to prepare for the second coming of Christ. At least four followers committed suicide.

5 This multinational soft drinks company organised a promotion lottery in which tops of bottles were stamped with numbers, some of which would enable the lucky owner to collect a prize equivalent to $40,000. However the computer had wrongly generated 800,000 of these numbers. They explained that they didn't have the $32 billion needed to pay all the claimants, and so merely offered the losers their apologies. When this fact was announced by the company there were violent protests in which one five-year-old girl was killed.

2 Punishing children

It would be convenient if there were an effective and suitable punishment to fit every childish crime. In theory, the punishment should fit the individual child, his age and his misdemeanour. In practice, even if it were possible to recommend this neat solution, actual punishments would continue to be influenced by variable and unpredictable factors. For example, a mother who smacks her child at the end of a long day is punishing him because she is tired and for all the irritating things he has done that day, not just for the trivial offence that finally provoked the slap. An outsider who saw only the isolated incident might think her harsh or unreasonable, but the child himself probably understands that the penalty covers a multitude of sins, and that his mother always gets bad-tempered around this time of a busy day.

1 Were you naughty as a child? How did your parents punish you?

2 Should parents use corporal punishment (slapping, smacking, belting, caning)?

3 Should anyone else other than the parents be allowed to smack a child?

4 Imagine that punishments did have to fit the crime. Think of some typical childish misdemeanours and how you would punish them.

5 How would you punish parents who abuse their children? Should their children be taken away from them?

Justice

3   Prisons

- Students read the first passage (A) and in groups discuss questions 1–4.

(i)   (1) & (2) If students lived in a small community and had to pay for the upkeep of the local prison from their own pockets (keeping a criminal in a prison is more expensive than paying for one to stay in a four star hotel), would they still send offenders to prison or would they come up with some valid alternative? (4) Answering this question entails firstly discussing why we have prisons (to lock people up and keep them out of harm's way, as a punishment, deterrent, for rehabilitation, because we've got nowhere else to put them). Students should also consider the causes of crime.

- Students now read the second passage and discuss questions 5 & 6, the answers to which are contained in the listening exercise below.

Listening

- Students hear about the prison experiment and answer these questions.

Questions: **1** How were the participants found and selected? **2** How long was the experiment supposed to last? **3** What happened after two days? **4** How did the 'guards' behave? And the 'prisoners'? **5** Why was the experiment stopped? **6** What did it supposedly prove? **7** What other explanation is there for the guards' behaviour?

🔑 **1** *newspaper advert; those considered most mentally and physically stable*   **2** *14 days*   **3** *rebellion + violent repression of the rebellion*   **4** *sadistically; after initial rebellion prisoners became submissive and emotional (some having to leave).*
5 *The head researcher's girlfriend had it stopped.*   **6** *That it is the environment that makes people aggressive ('the power of social and institutional forces to make good men engage in evil deeds').*   **7** *That participants were acting out stereotyped roles.*

📼 A … so they were fingerprinted, given a uniform and so on, just as if they were convicts in a real prison.

B But how did the researchers choose the pretend convicts and prison guards?

A They simply put an advertisement in a newspaper asking for male volunteers to take part in a psychological study of prison life. The ones they selected were the ones they reckoned were the most mentally and physically stable, and the most mature, actually the majority were middle class university students.

B And did they get any money for it?

A Well, they were they were supposed to get fifteen dollars a day for the two week period, and the ones that were selected to be prisoners were warned that they could expect to be under surveillance, they might be harassed, and they might have some of their basic rights curtailed during imprisonment.

B Not sure I would have agreed to do something like that, especially for two weeks.

A Well, in fact already within two days there was a rebellion, which the guards put down so severely that one prisoner began crying uncontrollably and screaming, and only after one day he had to be released and three others soon followed.

B So the guards really got into playing the part?

A Yeah, in fact as time passed, some of the guards seemed to derive great satisfaction from exercising power and acting really sadistically; they became more and more forceful and violent each day, despite the fact that most prisoners by this time had given up resisting. The guards even changed their mannerisms, like they began, they began swaggering around and the prisoners too began to slouch and keep their eyes fixed on the ground.

B God, it sounds so dehumanising. So then what happened?

A Well it was actually the chief researcher's girlfriend who put a stop to the whole thing. She'd gone to the prison to help out em interviewing the prisoners and she was so appalled and upset by what she saw that she pleaded with them to stop the experiment.

B Well, did the experiment prove anything after all this?

A Yeah, I suppose it did. I mean the people who took part were supposedly decent human beings with a good moral sense, I mean not deviants at all. So the researchers put down what happened to the environment.

B Yeah, but to a certain extent I suppose the guards were just acting like they supposed guards would act, I mean that's how we all see guards isn't it, as kinds of violent unthinking robots.

A Yes, yes, but that doesn't explain why the prisoners reacted so badly, I mean after all they knew that it was only an extended piece of role-playing.

B Well, all I can say is I hope to goodness I never end up in a prison.

4   The final judgement

- Students read the text and discuss the questions in groups. Students can compare the Bible's versions with their own religion's equivalent.

Justice

3 Prisons

A

In primitive societies wrongs were treated as private 'torts' rather than public 'crimes' and punishment was dealt out either by individual or group retaliation or by compensations — detection, conviction and punishment were in the hands of the whole community. Prisons haven't always existed, and even when they did they were not often used as they were too expensive to maintain.

In the 14th century, prisoners were expected to provide all their own necessities — food, drink, bedding, clothing, even candles and fuel for fire. If you wanted a separate room you had to pay for it, and if you didn't have enough money to buy the food and beer from your gaoler's shop, you might even die of starvation or thirst.

Certainly the most economical form of punishment is execution, but with the advent of a more humanitarian society other less drastic forms were invented. In the 1820s and 1830s, for example, around 4000 criminals a year were transported from Britain to Australia. Increased government revenue around this time made a prison system possible, which made the grading of punishment considerably easier — weeks, months and years, rather than ears, arms and legs.

B

A group of social psychologists were interested in determining the causes of the dehumanisation that is so prevalent in prisons. Suppose that ordinary members of society were persuaded to act as guards and prisoners in a mock prison which mimicked the environment and day-to-day running of a real prison? If the mock prison failed to produce the hostility and alienation of a real prison, this would surely suggest that the personality characteristics of the guards or the prisoners, or both, are the vital ingredients in the unpleasantness found in a real prison. On the other hand, if the behaviour observed in the mock prison was very similar to that in a real prison, this would suggest that it is the environment of a prison which is the crucial factor in producing unpleasantness.

1 What are prison conditions like in your country?

2 What are the pros and cons of detection, conviction and punishment being in the hands of the whole community?

3 Would having to pay to stay in prison be a good deterrent in modern society?

4 Imagine that prisons were abolished, what could be used in their place?

5 How do you think the researchers (extract B) carried out their experiment and what was the result?

6 How do you think the 'guards' and the 'prisoners' reacted?

4 The final judgement

1 What evidence can you see or feel in the world around you for and against an idea of ultimate justice?

2 How would you answer Jeremiah's questions?

3 Is it right that some people are born rich, intelligent and beautiful, and others poor, stupid and ugly?

4 Is your life predestined by the country where you are born and the parents who you are born to?

5 Is it fair that we only live once? Or do we only live once?

6 Should famous people be sentenced more severely than others to set an example?

Then I saw a great white throne and the one who sits on it. And I saw the dead, great and small alike, standing before the throne. Books were opened, and then another book was opened, the book of the living. The dead were judged according to what they had done, as recorded in the books. Whoever did not have his name written in the book of the living was thrown into the lake of fire.

The Book of Revelations 20, 11–15

Lord, if I argued my case with you, you would prove to be right. Yet I must question you about matters of justice. Why are wicked men so prosperous? Why do dishonest men succeed? You plant them, and they take root; they grow and bear fruit.

Jeremiah questions the Lord, *Jeremiah 12, 1–2*

Kids

Warm-up

- The Kidz quiz is probably the best way to start the lesson. Alternatively you could give students this baby test. **1** How much does the average baby weigh at birth? **2** When does a baby normally start consuming food other than milk? **3** When do babies generally start walking? **4** What is normally a baby's first word and when can they really start talking? **5** When do babies stop wearing nappies?

🔑 *1 In a developed country the average boy weighs around 3.2 kg (girls a little less).   2 After a few months babies can have milk mixed with pureed cereals and fruit, by their first birthday some are already joining in with a variation on the normal family meal. 3 At around 6 months some babies begin picking themselves up, then they begin to walk with support, and then between 12 and 18 months they're really walking.   4 A variation on the word 'mummy' (though I'm proud to say that my child's first word was 'daddy'!), by the age of two, kids have a vocabulary of around 300 words, and 5000 at five.   5 Usually some time between eighteen months and three years.*

- Dictate the following list or elicit by a brainstorming session on what they associate with childhood: toys, brothers and sisters, pets, best friend, food likes and dislikes, TV, parents, teachers, wishes, holidays, beliefs etc.
- Now get them to do a bit of childhood reminiscing using the above subjects as a basis. What things do they miss about their childhood? What don't they miss at all? Are children becoming maturer at an early age? What are the implications of this?

1   Kidz quiz

- Students first do question **1**. At the same time they analyse how children are different from adults, in terms of general behaviour, inter-personal relationships, needs, wishes, creativity, curiosity etc. The adjectives are supposed to be antonyms (to some extent), so encourage students to find the opposites. Get feedback, after which you might like to use questions **2** and **3** as a class discussion; or if you think they would be too difficult, tell students to begin their discussion of the other questions from question **4**. In multilingual classes it might be interesting to get some more class feedback on some of the questions. Discussion of the last few questions should then lead nicely on to **Parents**.

🔑 *(Suggested answers to 1, others may be possible): Antonyms: cautious – fearless; curious – indifferent; dull – imaginative; easy to please – intolerant; funny – serious; innocent – tainted; narrow-minded – open-minded; predictable – spontaneous; sour – sweet*

2   Parents

- NB Only use this section with more mature students, use one of the two **warm-ups** as an alternative.
- Brainstorm students on why men and women have children. Do they have the same reasons for wanting them? How and why does society pressurise married couples to have children? Why are other people (e.g. single people, unmarried couples, homosexual couples) frowned upon if they have children?
- Students read the text. Give them the information below. They then read the questions 1–10 and match them to the three section headings – two of the section headings have three associated questions each, the other one has four. Students may decide that some questions are relevant to more than one heading – they can discuss this. With an older group these questions can be discussed along with the idea of 'selfishness' outlined below in the **Info**.

ⓘ BON is a support group of people from a wide spectrum of social and cultural backgrounds, parents and non-parents, who feel the need of an organisation to promote and protect the interests, needs and wishes of those who have chosen, adjusted to, or support being childfree. In a world with over five billion inhabitants the option not to be a parent should be carefully considered by anyone contemplating the irrevocable decision to have a child. In a society that expresses a very one-sided view of the 'joys of parenthood', it is regarded as selfish to opt for a life without children. But surely the motives behind having a child can be just as 'selfish'? It has been established that a large proportion of child abuse arises out of the unreal expectations held by many parents. What can be more selfish than the person who says 'I don't care about overpopulation, food shortages, or pollution. I don't care to consider whether I will make a good parent. I want a child no matter what it costs to society, myself, my marriage and my child'.

🔑 *1A 2C 3C 4B 5B 6A 7A 8C 9C 10B*

1 Kidz quiz

1 Decide which adjectives are appropriate for describing children and which ones for adults. Give reasons.

cautious	imaginative	predictable
curious	indifferent	serious
dull	innocent	sour, bitter, dry
easy to please	intolerant	spontaneous
fearless	narrow-minded	sweet
funny	open-minded	tainted

2 Children should be seen and not heard. (English saying)

3 Children should not eat with their parents, nor be allowed into restaurants.

4 From the age of six children should help to do the housework.

5 Children under the age of 10 should be in bed by 7.30 p.m.

6 It is up to the parents to decide how their children should dress.

7 Children should be allowed to have a TV in their bedroom.

8 The more pocket money you give a child, the more responsible they become.

9 Children cannot decide for themselves what friends to have.

10 Parents have the right to keep their children at home to work, rather than send them to school.

2 Parents

In our society a high value is placed on 'parenthood at any price' rather than on responsible parenthood for those who freely choose it without being pressurised. Most couples are inevitably asked 'When are we going to hear the patter of tiny feet?' and other such comments as soon as they are married. The media, and especially advertising constantly push the message that having children is fun, natural and necessary. There is a strong implication that if you do not conform, there is something wrong with you! The question everyone should ask themselves is not 'Why don't I ...?,' but 'Why do I want a child?'

In the box below are 10 questions from a questionnaire prepared by the British Organisation of Non-parents (BON). The questions were organised under three headings:

A **What sort of a parent would I be?**

B **Would a child fit into my way of life?**

C **What do I expect to gain from the experience of being a parent?**

Your task is to match the questions with the titles and then to decide whether choosing not to have children is selfish or not.

---

1 What do I know about discipline and freedom? Would I be too strict? Too lenient? Would I get upset if things weren't perfect?

2 Would I expect my child to do all the things I wished I had done?

3 Am I happy playing Monopoly all afternoon – even though I am bored after one game – or leaving the Zoo after ten minutes – even though it cost us £15.00 to get in?

4 Could I handle children and work? Do I have plenty of energy at the end of the day or am I tired?

5 Would I have to give up interests and activities I feel important to me?

6 What kind of relationship do I have with my own parents? Would I want to have the same relationship with my children?

7 Do I like children? Have I had enough contact with babies? toddlers? teenagers?

8 Would I expect a baby to make my marriage complete?

9 What would I do if my child had ideas and beliefs different from mine? How different?

10 Would I be willing and happy to restrict my social life? Would I miss lost leisure time and privacy?

3 Adoption

- Begin by brainstorming the question of what couples who are unable to have children can do to resolve their problem. This will probably lead you on to a discussion on adoption but may also elicit artificial insemination and surrogacy.
- Students read the ad, discuss why the couple wrote it, and the possible implications. Then discuss the questions.

Listening

- Students hear about adoption in Britain. Students predict the answers to these questions before listening.
  Questions: 1 What percentage of adopted children are under the age of one? 2 What has changed in the last 30 years? 3 Which are the biggest and second biggest age groups for adoption (1–4, 5–9, 10–14, 15–18)? And the percentages? 4 What colour adoptive parents should black children be given to? 5 Which kind of children most need adopting but are least likely to find adoptive parents? 6 What is the woman's hope for the future?

🔑 1 *10%* 2 *Attitudes to and pressures on unmarried mothers.* 3 *5–9 (33%), 10–14 (20%)* 4 *Black.* 5 *Handicapped and victims of parental abuse.* 6 *That more people will adopt children to help someone who really needs love and attention.*

Most people still seem to have the idea that adoption is about a couple, who can't have their own children, going to an agency, being given a virtually new-born child, and then taking it home and bringing it up. About thirty years ago it may have been like that. The fact is that now only about ten per cent of children adopted are under one year of age. In Britain, at least, this is due to the fact that attitudes have changed and unmarried mothers now keep their children, that is unless they haven't already decided to abort beforehand. There used to be a lot of pressure on women like this to give up their baby, but now there isn't. The biggest age group is in fact from five to nine, and about a third of adopted children fall into this group. And ten to fourteen year olds are the next biggest group – representing about twenty per cent of the total number. People, well, at least white people, also tend to think of adopting healthy white children. But by far the majority of children for adoption are neither one nor the other. A lot are black children, who if possible are adopted by black parents. This is because a child needs parents who share the child's cultural heritage. It's much easier for the child if the new parents have the same religious background and language, attitude and customs as the child's birth parents would have done. Adopted children need to retain a sense of their own identity, which would be difficult if they were brought up by white parents with a completely different background. The sad thing is that a lot of the children who really need a new family are the least likely to get one. I'm talking about handicapped children, both mentally and physically, and of course those who were abused by their parents. Very few people, understandably I suppose, are prepared to take on a child with a disability or a child who might totally disrupt their life with a whole host of problems derived from the birth parents. My hope is that in the future more people will adopt children, not as a substitute for the one they couldn't have themselves, but simply to help someone who really needs their love and attention.

4 Children and ethics

💣 Test the ground before starting this topic. Some of your students might not wish to discuss it.

Listening

- Play the extract once and then get students to read the five cases 1–5. Get them to note down which situation (🔑 2) was being talked about. Play the extract again, and ask if the male speaker was for or against conceiving the child. Then in groups get them to summarise the speaker's argument and then continue the discussion themselves.
- Now let each group choose two more situations to talk about. Finally, get them to match the situations with the information a–d. For situation 4, get students to discuss the pros and cons of the operation on the assumption that the operation is successful from a medical point of view, i.e. there are no problems of rejection because the toe is re-attached to the person who it is taken from.

🔑 1*d* 2 *(discussed in listening)* 3*b* 4*a* 5*c*

A .... so they had to do it themselves.
B Wow! Actually that reminds me of that couple who needed a donor for their child, a little girl I think she was, to give her some transplant or other. They waited for so long that in the end the mother decided to have another child, and she was in her forties I seem to remember, and ...
A They operated on the new baby I suppose.
B Yeah that's right, and the little baby managed to save the life of her sister.
A You know I'm not sure I agree with that kind of thing.
B What do you mean?
A Like suppose they'd analysed the fetus of this baby and the test showed that the tissue wasn't compatible for transplant, I mean, do they abort and try again?
B Yeah, I hadn't thought about that.
A And you know is it right to conceive a child, subject it to some operation, without ever asking it how it feels about all this? In any case it seems a bit of a strange reason to want a child, just for the sake of ...
B Yeah but Al, people have babies for much less serious reasons, which may be totally frivolous, sentimental or whatever. Some folks have kids just so that when they grow up they can work for them, you know like on farms. I mean supposing that they'd just said — OK we're going to have another child so that, Meryl, or whatever the kid's name was, can have a little sister — you know nobody would have said anything. I mean it's ironic that people can do that, but they're not supposed to have a child to save another child's life. Well, don't you think?

3 Adoption

> **ADOPTION** Loving white couple, young and financially secure, long to provide a warm and caring home for your baby. We lead a quiet lifestyle, and we enjoy sports and other outdoor activities. All expenses paid legally and confidentially. Please call Kate and Jerry collect at 555-3467.

1 Would you adopt even if you could have, or already have, your own children?

2 Why might some couples prefer to have children which are biologically their own? Why do other couples choose to adopt?

3 If you want to adopt a child, do you think you have the right to choose your own child (i.e. choose the age, sex and race)? Would you consider adopting a handicapped child?

4 When should parents tell the child that he/she was adopted?

5 Where possible, should the adoptive parents maintain contact with the natural parents? Should the natural parents be allowed to visit their child?

6 Should the adoptive parents try to let their child be aware of and interested in his/her original cultural background?

4 Children and ethics

1 These six women wish to have an abortion. (a) 26, unmarried and is pregnant after a casual relationship. (b) 45, not very wealthy, married and already has five children. (c) A 16-year-old girl who has been raped. (d) 35, married, doesn't want children and believes that having a child would destroy her career, her husband however would like a child. (e) Stands a 50% chance of dying herself if she gives birth. (f) Married, and pregnant after a one-off extra-marital relationship with someone of a different colour skin.

2 These parents wish to conceive a child in order to obtain an organ to save the life of another of their children.

3 This physician from a mental institution wishes to sterilise a sexually precocious 15-year-old girl who is severely mentally retarded and has already had two abortions.

4 This doctor wants to transplant children's toes to their hands to create fingers, for those who have been born without fingers or have lost them in an accident.

5 These parents have 3-year-old Siamese twins, with two heads but only one set of arms and legs. They want advice about separating the children.

a Mr Kay, an English surgeon, has successfully transplanted a total of 32 toes, on to 22 patients with a 100% success rate. Some parents reject this system as being a further mutilation of the child, but Mr Kay quotes the case of an 8-year-old girl who had only one finger on one hand. By transplanting a toe she was provided with a thumb, and within months she was able to dress herself for the first time.

b In 1992 the European Parliament passed a resolution giving parents the permission to decide to sterilise their mentally handicapped children. But the consequences of the abuse of sterilisation call to mind the Spartans and Hitler. Churchill, in his early years as an MP, wanted to sterilise non-productive and immoral members of British society.

c An Irish couple, faced with this dilemma, separated the children, but one of them died.

d There are 1.6m abortions carried out in the U.S. each year, representing almost one-fourth of all pregnancies. More than 46% of American women will probably have had one by the time they are 45. Many militant 'pro-life' groups issue death threats to doctors who provide abortions.

Language

Warm-up

- Get students to try reading the tongue twisters on their page.

Listening

- Students hear some people trying to do the tongue twisters. Their task is to decide if they are said correctly or not.

🔊 **1** *She sells ... (OK)*   **2** *Double ... (OK)*   **3** *Is there ... (OK)*   **4** *Are you aluminiming them my man no I'm copperbottoming them mum mum*   **5** *The stinking steamer stank.*   **6** *The sick sixth sheep sick sheep's sick.*   **7** *Around the rogged rocks a rogged rascal rin.*

1   As simple as A B C

- Students look at the Chinese ideograms. Get them to guess what the ideograms represent, then brainstorm students on the difficulties of learning and speaking Chinese.

🔊 **a** *hand*   **b** *eye*   **c** *see*   **d** *lesson*

Listening

- Students hear part of an interview with a Chinese woman talking about her language (point out that she is multilingual). Get them to prepare a list of their own questions, and then to see if any are answered in the listening. Alternatively, after hearing each extract, ask students to write down a possible question for each answer. With lower levels, give students the questions below. They listen to hear the order in which the questions were answered.

Questions: **a** Of all the languages you've learned, which is the most difficult?   **b** Has the written language changed much over the centuries?   **c** What connection is there between the written and the spoken language?   **d** Does the fact that it's a visual language influence the way you think?   **e** Will China ever adopt a Western script? And would this be a good idea?   **f** How big are the keyboards needed to type in Chinese?   **g** What have you learned by knowing so many languages?

🔊 **1f   2a   3c   4b   5e   6d   7g**

📼 1 Um, it's bigger than the normal one apart from the fact that we there are a lot of softwares on the computer which make use of phonetic transcription, the sound. They search by sound, so you don't need a particular keyboard. But typical typewriters are actually quite big and you can change the keyboard two or three times and it's quite difficult and quite cumbersome.

2 I would still say Chinese even if it's my first mother tongue. Yes, apart from difficulty in learning it, it's difficult to keep it, to remember that. I mean, if you stop using it for some time you do forget it.

3 They are two different things. So, the percentage of people who, of Chinese, who cannot write anything, it's very high, because you can never connect, associate the pronunciation with the word, so you simply don't know the word and there's no element to help you, to imagine how a word can be written if you don't, if you haven't learned that word.

4 Yes, because under Mao, he invented a system, a, a, a new sort of handwriting, which is simplified, quite simpler, but it is also quite confusing to Chinese living abroad, I mean, outside mainland China.

5 If it will ever happen it will happen in the very, very, very far away future, not right now. I think it wouldn't be that good if you want to maintain the culture of China, because Chinese language is typical because it is visual and all the old poetry, for example, depends a lot on the words as they are written.

6 We tend more to think in, if you can say that, in images too, and not only in words and; we tend to associate things with the sounds that we hear.

7 I do believe that in the learning the language you also learn, how how people from that country think, how they behave, and you learn part of their culture.

2   Do you speak Esperanto?

- Having done **As simple as A B C**, students should now be able to decide on what targets to set for an ideal language. Tell them to think of the five most important things an ideal language should have (or not have): if they need help tell them to think in terms of vocabulary, use of articles, tenses etc.
- Get class feedback and write their suggestions on the board. Elicit Esperanto, by asking them if they know of any artificial languages. Get them to write down three questions that they'd like answered about Esperanto (these may then be answered in the listening below).

Listening

- Students hear a few facts about Esperanto. They simply check whether their questions were answered. Alternatively, after the first listening, students write their own questions (as many as possible) which they then pass to their partner who has to answer such questions after the second listening. (The tapescript is on page 54.)
- Students read the descriptions of Esperanto on their page. They should go through each element critically, deciding if it matches their own targets and whether it represents an improvement on existing languages.

ⓘ (1) Is this communication on an equal footing? (2) Why have accents? They are problematic and cause difficulties when typing. (3) Do we need an indefinite article? Do we need articles at all? (4) Is this really necessary? (5) Unnecessarily complicated by consistency. (6) Couldn't intonation replace cû? (7) Most languages do without them. (8) Which is more logical – English or Esperanto (and most other languages)? (9) This leads on to the question of translation, which is covered in the next section.

1 As simple as A B C

1 Is English easier or more difficult than your native language? Why and how?

2 Compare English with any other language you have had to learn, in terms of grammar, spelling and pronunciation.

3 How should foreign languages be taught in schools? What should be the typical elements of a good lesson?

4 Should foreign languages be taught in schools in America, Australia and Britain?

5 When you learn a foreign language, apart from the language what else do you learn about?

1 **She sells sea shells on the sea shore, the shells she sells are sea shells I'm sure.**

2 **Double bubble gum bubbles double.**

3 *Is there a pleasant pheasant present?*

4 **Are you aluminuming my man? No I'm copper bottoming them Mum.**

5 **The sinking steamer sunk.**

6 **The sick sixth sheik's sheep's sick.**

7 *Around the ragged rocks the ragged rascal ran.*

a 手 b 目 c 看 d 课

2 Do you speak Esperanto?

1 Esperanto words come from the most important languages in Western civilisation, mainly from Latin. Some words look exactly as they do in English, for example *birdo* (a bird), *rivero* (a river); others, such as *mano* (hand) come from Latin.

2 Esperanto is phonetic, there are only five vowel sounds. The stress is always on the penultimate syllable. Six of the letters have accents (e.g. ĉ, ĥ).

3 There is no indefinite article: *patro* = a father or just father. The definite article, 'la', is used with all nouns, masculine and feminine, singular and plural: *la filo* = the son, *la filoj* = the sons.

4 Subjects and objects are distinguished, by adding '-n' to the object: *la viro amas la virinon* (the man loves the woman); if you reverse the order (*la virinon amas la viro*) the meaning remains the same. The same rule applies to make the distinction between 'who' and 'whom'.

5 Adjectives must agree with the noun they qualify: *novaj tabloj* (new tables); adjectives are placed either before or after the noun with no change in meaning.

6 All verbs are regular (to be = *mi estas, li estas, si estas, vi estas, ni estas, ili estas*), and to form questions put 'ĉu' before the affirmative form: *ĉu vi estas?* (Are you?)

7 There are no continuous forms: *mi legas* = I read and I am reading (depending on the context). Other tenses are formed by adding suffixes to the root word. Indirect speech uses the same tense as in direct speech.

8 Esperanto uses the present tense to translate sentences like: I have been ill for three days. He has been waiting for two hours.

9 Names of countries are written with capital letters, but not the inhabitants, nor the days of the week. Some of the more important, larger cities have names in Esperanto: *Parizo, Vieno, Manĉestro*; some just take '-o': *Londono, Madrido*; others remain the same especially if they are difficult to Esperantise: *Versailles, Bournemouth*. Foreign words are adapted to conform to the Esperanto spelling system.

1	unu (oo-noo)
2	du (doo)
3	tri (tree)
4	kvar
5	kvin
6	ses
7	sep
8	ok
9	nau (now)
10	dek
100	cent (tsent)
1000	mil (meel)

Language

3 Translation

- In groups students discuss those words in their language that they find difficult to translate and for which they believe there is no direct English equivalent (e.g. the French 'sympathique'). In monolingual classes students produce a list of four or five of such words and together try and find the nearest English equivalent. They should then discuss possible reasons why English has no word for that particular concept. Then get feedback from whole class and suggest your own translations where necessary.
- In multilingual classes, group different nationalities together. Each student explains the meaning of one word for which he/she believes there is no equivalent, the others suggest possible translations. Then get feedback from whole class and suggest your own translations where necessary.
- In groups students now discuss why we need translations.
- Now ask them to read the passage, without giving them any indication as to what the passage is about. When they have finished reading ask them if they found anything strange about it (they should at least have found it amusing and spotted some English mistakes). Now get them to underline any examples of irony (e.g. 'incredible to think', 'it's obvious isn't it', 'obviously', 'moving'), and any mistakes in the English and in the spelling. Finally, ask them to rewrite Carolino's dedication into good English (not an easy task); you should prepare your own version to read to them.
- Students now define the meaning of translation – what does translation involve? What types of work are generally translated? To help them in their discussion, they should decide whether the sentences on their page are true or false.

Writing

- Students write on one of these subjects: (a) Translation is a valuable aid to language teaching. Discuss. (b) Translation is a science not an art. Discuss. Alternatively give students a translation to do.

Useful further reading:
Alan Duff: *The third language*;
Peter Newmark: *Approaches to translation*.

4 Sign language

- Brainstorm students on other means of communication besides written and spoken language. Elicit body and sign language.
- Brainstorm them on what the various signs on their page mean, and who they are for (i.e. the deaf). If this draws a blank, tell students that the signs illustrate the following concepts: America, disagree, doubt, dream, must, silly. In groups, see if students can match the words with the signs.

🔊 a *America* b *must* c *doubt* d *dream* e *silly* f *disagree*

ⓘ The rationale behind the America sign, is that the meshed fingers represent the United States. Another explanation is that the fingers represent a log cabin.

Listening

- Students hear two people describing how to make the signs. Students' task is to match the descriptions with the signs. NB The first two listening pieces could be used as an alternative introduction to the whole exercise. Play the first piece and get students to actually do what the speaker tells them to do, not all students will follow the instructions in the same way. Then brainstorm the students on what they think the purpose of the exercise is – they may think it's part of a fitness programme!

🔊 1*b* 2*d* 3*a* 4*f*

📼 1 Hold, hold up both arms and extend your arms slightly in front of you with your hands flat and your palms facing inwards, then move your arms up and down.

2 Hold your right arm out to the side, bend it at the elbow, and keep your three middle fingers extended, and fairly straight, your baby finger and your thumb should be down touching the palm of your hand. Then with a slightly curly movement, spiral almost, bring it to your forehead over your right eye and back again.

3 This person's standing with their hands in front of them, their fingers intertwined, and then with the thumbs pointing upwards, and then moving the thumbs around in circles.

4 They're standing again with their hands in front of them, but this time their fingers clenched and thumbs up, em holding their hands in front of their chest, and then moving them out and opening the palms out, away from their body and opening the palms.

Tapescript for 2 Do you speak Esperanto?

📼 Esperanto was first published in 1887 by a Polish oculist, Dr Ludovic Zamenhof, under the pseudonym 'Dr Esperanto', meaning 'one who hopes'. He believed that world peace would only come if we all spoke the same language, which would allow communication on an equal footing, without one speaker having a cultural advantage over the other. Zamenhof devised Esperanto in Russia, where four languages were commonly spoken at the time. He spent years diligently concocting his language. Luckily he was a determined fellow because at an advanced stage in the work his father, fearing his son would be thought a spy working in code, threw all Ludovic's papers on the fire and the young Pole was forced to start again from scratch. Zamenhof was actually not the only one inventing an artificial universal language of communication, between 1880 and 1907, another 53 were invented. But Esperanto was the simplest of all, with a basis of just 16 rules. Some Esperantists claim to have eight million adherents in 110 countries, but the World Almanac puts the number of speakers at two million. Esperanto teachers say that with three hours of study a week it can be mastered in a year.

3 Translation

One of the most infamous translations of all times was in the writing of a trilingual edition of familiar phrases. The first edition, published in 1836, was in French and Portuguese. It sold so well that the publishers decided to bring out a version with English too. They thus engaged the services of a certain Pedro Carolino. The only problem was that Pedro didn't know a word of English, he merely used a French-English dictionary to do the job!

This soon becomes obvious when we read, for example in the 'Degrees of Kindred' section, such mistakes as 'A relation', 'An relation'; 'A widower', 'An widow'. It is incredible to think that until Pedro Carolino came along, no-one, not even the Englishes themselves, had realised that just like the French and Portuguese and Spanish and Italyan, English is a language with genders.

Once he's pointed it out to you it's obvious, isn't it, that 'A relation' is masculine and 'An relation' feminine. A further step in turning English into a Romance language is taken by making the possessive pronouns agree with their accompanying nouns both in gender and number. Thus the word 'nails', being plural and feminine (obviously), must be accompanied by a plural feminine pronoun — the result being, for example, 'He has scratched the face with her nails.'

Carolino ends the preface to his book with this moving dedication:

'We expect then, who the little book (for the care what we wrote him and for her typographical correction) that may be worth the acceptation of the studious persons, and especially of the Youth, at which we dedicate him particularly.'

1 A translator must think about the intent of the writer and the types of reader.

2 Every word should be translated and the original word order should be kept to as close as possible.

3 Names of people, towns and institutions should not be translated, nor should titles of works of art.

4 Idiomatic phrases should be translated literally.

5 The style of the original should be kept as much as possible.

6 The original structure and layout should remain intact.

7 Book and film titles should be translated literally or not at all.

8 There is no point trying to translate poetry.

9 It is better to read a book or watch a film in the original language, subtitles are preferable to dubbing.

10 Automatic translation using computers will eventually replace human translation.

4 Sign language

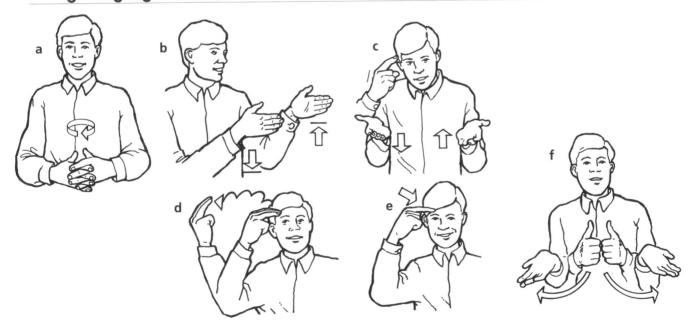

Memory

Warm-ups

- Put 20 objects/photocards (perhaps related to a particular lexical set you want to practise) on a tray. Cover the tray after one minute, students then have two minutes to write the objects they remember. Get students to guess the topic of today's lesson. Skip the next activity.
- Put students in pairs back to back. They have to describe what each is wearing. Students analyse why such an apparently easy task is so difficult.
- Write the following words on the board (or elicit from students): forget, memo(randum), memorable, memories, memorise, memory, memento, nostalgia, recall, recollect, recollections, remember, remind, reminder, reminiscence, unforgettable. Get students to prepare a chart with three headings (verb, noun, adjective) and ask them to put the words into the appropriate columns. Then as a whole class, analyse the differences between the various words. Alternatively, give each group a pair/set of words (e.g. memorise/remember/remind; memories/memory; memory/nostalgia/ reminiscence) the same word can appear in more than one set. Each group analyses their own particular set and then reports back to the class.

1   I remember your name perfectly but I just can't think of your face

- Brainstorm students on what we need memory for. What would happen if we lost our memory?
- Move on to student's page. Check that students understand the meaning of the quotation. They then answer the questions.

(i)   The title of this section is a quotation from Rev. Spooner (1844–1930), an Oxford don famous for muddling words up. His name has given rise to the word 'spoonerism'. When announcing the hymn in New College Chapel in 1879 he said: 'Kinquering Congs their titles take'; and when dismissing a student: 'You have deliberately tasted two worms and you can leave Oxford by the town drain'. (4) A logical reason might simply be that the visual information we have on first seeing an object gets mistakenly sent to the wrong place (where it is subconsciously registered), before arriving at the correct place (where it is consciously registered). So we have actually seen the place before, but only milliseconds before, not in a dream or another life.

2   Mental filing system

- If you think the passage has interest value, ask students to read it and discuss any other implications of ignoring information that doesn't conform to our filing system. If not, in groups, students read all the questions then choose and propose one question they'd like to discuss.

Writing

- Students choose one of these titles: (a) Is it more important for an individual or for a nation not to forget the past? (b) Is a memory sometimes better than the real thing?

Listening

- There are two aims to this listening exercise. One is as a straightforward test of comprehension, and the other is to promote further discussion on memory.
- Play the tape once, giving students the following instructions. (The tapescript is on page 58.) You are going to listen to twins (Jo and Ed) who talk about the same event. Your task is to spot the differences between the way the twins remember what happened. Explain what the FWA (see script) is and how tides work.
- All but the best students will find this task rather difficult – as a whole class discuss why. Possible reasons: the piece is rather long (but is nevertheless typical of many advanced level listening exercises); students were probably unable to memorise the information, due both to lack of concentration (along with a degree of boredom probably!), and to the fact that they were given no tools to help them in the exercise.
- Now play the piece again, but write the following table on the board (without the answers!) for students to fill in.

	JO	ED
age	10	12
FWA involvement	yes	no
level of fear	doesn't remember	Jo was petrified; was scared too but tried not to show it
tide	out	in
part of body water reached	waist	chest
why rescuer came	dog	boys
return visit	yes	no

- Check answers; students will have found that they understood much more. Why? You have to create a kind of framework to store the information you receive; perhaps memory techniques should be taught in school – what do your students think? What techniques do they use?

(i)   We tend to remember better the beginnings and endings of things (films, books, jokes, even words and sentences) – this means it is important not to lose concentration in the middle of reading and listening exercises. Studies have also proved that we remember things better if we put them in a meaningful context; for instance, it is easier to remember a long complex but meaningful sentence than a short, simple meaningless one – this obviously has implications for vocabulary learning.

1   I remember your name perfectly, but I just can't think of your face.

1 How good are you at remembering names, dates, facts for exams, books, films, appointments, lists, speeches, anecdotes, jokes, etc.? What techniques do you use?

2 Why do we remember some people and forget others? Why are we embarrassed about forgetting people's names? Do you assume that people will remember you?

3 Do you buy souvenirs when you go to new places? Do you take photographs to remind you of places and people?

4 Do you ever have a sense of déjà vu? How do you explain this phenomenon?

5 Is it easier to remember or to forget?

6 What methods do people use to record their memories (diaries, photo-albums, videos etc.)?

2   Mental filing system

1 What is your earliest memory?

2 What would happen if we couldn't forget?

3 Do you like listening to old people recounting their favourite memories?

4 Have you ever forgotten to do something really important?

5 Have you ever had to re-adjust your mental filing system to accept things that perhaps it didn't want to?

6 Do we tend to rewrite or distort our past when we look back on it (perhaps to make it conform to the way we see things now or think we should see things)?

7 If you could have your own mental waste-paper basket, what would you put in it?

8 What are the possible uses of a photographic memory?

9 Would you like to literally physically swap memories with someone?

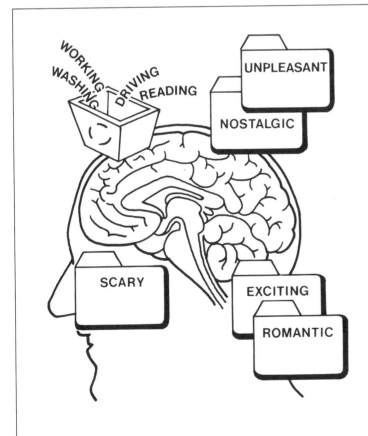

Exactly how our memories work is still something of a mystery. Why is it, for example, that we remember very little of what happened to us before we were three or four? One theory is that the place in the brain where we store our memories, the hippocampus, has not yet fully developed its filing system.

An analogy with a filing system is useful because it can help us to understand why we forget, or appear to forget, certain awkward or painful events. These events may simply not have been filed, or were quickly shifted from our short term in-tray to be hidden away in our long term memory. This is helpful when we may have experienced something very painful (childbirth, rejection in love), which we need to have forgotten before embarking on a similar experience.

Unfortunately, we may also have a tendency to ignore information that doesn't fit neatly into our filing system. Before coming to England for the first time, you may think that all English people are polite, orderly and reserved, and that the food is disgusting. When you actually get to England, you may tend to only look for things that confirm this idea, ignoring the fact that many English people are far from being reserved, and that English food is really quite delicious!

3 Improve your memory

- This is essentially a reading exercise. Students discuss equivalents that they have in their own languages. If you are going to use the geometrical symbols exercise, make sure this is covered while students are reading the texts.
- Students look at the geometrical figures for 30 seconds, then try to reproduce them in the same order. Alternatively, pre-teach language connected with geometrical figures. Allow one set of students only to see the top row and the others the bottom row. They study their pictures for 30 seconds, and then have to dictate what they remember to their partner.

Extra

- Read out the pairs of words opposite allowing about a two-second pause between each word. Students have to remember the pairs from the first column simply by mentally repeating them as they hear them, the second set by inventing a sentence which in some way connects them and the third set by some kind of visual association between the two words. In each case the speaker repeats the first word of each pair and students have to write down the second word.

(i) Most people find the first set the most difficult, then the second, with best results in the third. Perhaps students should bear this in mind when learning new vocabulary in English.

chair-cloud	radio-hand	snake-bath
glass-ball	shoe-river	clock-boat
pen-cigarette	house-paper	nose-garage
box-star	knife-flower	king-car
church-egg	salt-carrot	fish-computer
girl-book	film-candle	octopus-plane
milk-train	sofa-bicycle	cow-bridge

Tapescript for 2 Mental filing system

Jo We always used to go on holiday to Trearddur Bay which is on a little island off Anglesey in Wales. Well one day we set off for a walk, together as usual, because I mean we were inseparable at that age, I guess we must have been nine or ten, and we went to a place called the Inland Sea which is a kind of beachy boggy area which is covered when the tide comes in, but which you can walk across when the tide is out. We'd never been on this walk before so we asked two local Welsh boys who happened to be there which was the best way to get across, you know, from one side to the other, and they told us which way, and off we set. Well if we'd been a little older and a little wiser we would never have listened to those two boys. The thing was that at that time, there was something called the FWA – the Free Wales Army – a Welsh nationalist group. Well, anyway they'd really got it in for any English family who'd got, as we had, a holiday house on the island. In fact, that summer several holiday houses had been set on fire. So anyway what the two Welsh boys had assured us was a safe way across turned out to be a nightmare. We'd got about half way across when we found ourselves in quicksand and we started sinking slowly into the sand up to our waists. I don't actually remember being scared at all, I don't think either of us was aware of the danger of it all. And luckily the tide was still going out, so at least there was no real threat of being covered by the sea water, at least not for another six hours. You know I don't even remember screaming for help, but anyway we were actually discovered by a dog that came sniffing up to us and then went back for its owner, who was another holidaymaker I

think, who ran across to us, hauled me out first and then Edward. D'you know, I remember that the thing that really upset me was that my nice new wellingtons were left stuck in the sandy mud. And the next day I went back on my own to see if I could find them, but I couldn't pluck up the courage to walk over to where we'd got stuck, which was just as well I suppose.

Ed We were about, well about twelve at the time I think, and we were on this walk at the Inland Sea, which I presume my sister has described for you. She has. OK. Well we'd been told by these two local lads that there was a quick way to get across. We needed a quick way because we were already late as it was and my parents were expecting us back home for lunch. Anyway, anyway we'd hardly got started when we began sinking in this quicksand. Joanna was petrified and so was I though I tried not to show it though. And the thing was that the tide was coming in, and although it does take a long time to actually come in, it probably wouldn't have reached us for an hour or so, I was imagining it coming up over our heads. Actually the sand only came up to well just below our chests in the end, but you can imagine how scary it was. By this time the sand had come right up to our chests so it was pretty scary. Joanna's always been convinced that the two boys were out to get us, but I don't think so; anyway one of them must have seen what was going on because after about ten minutes or so a man came rushing over, it was a holidaymaker like us I think, because he knew our parents. Anyway he came over with his dog and he pulled us out, first my sister and then me. I seem to remember that all Jo could think about was her wellingtons that had got stuck in the mud. Anyway the man then took us home to our parents, and they went white when they heard the story, and we've never been back since.

3 Improve your memory

One way for remembering simple pieces of information
(chemical formulas, historical dates and rulers, geographical
facts and figures) is to use a mnemonic (Mnemosyne was the
Greek goddess of memory).

Months:

Thirty days has September

April, June and November

All the rest have thirty one

Excepting February alone

Which has twenty eight days clear

And twenty nine in each leap year.

The weather:
Red sky at night
shepherd's delight,
red sky in the morning
shepherd's warning.

For drinkers:
**Beer on whisky very risky,
whisky on beer never fear.**

Zodiac signs:

Our vernal signs the Ram begins	Aries
Then comes the bull, in May the twins,	Taurus, Gemini
The Crab in June, next Leo shines,	Cancer, Leo
And Virgo ends the northern signs.	Virgo
The Balance brings autumnal fruits,	Libra
The Scorpian stings, the Archer shoots;	Scorpio, Sagittarius
December's Goat brings wintry blast	Capricorn
Aquarius rain, the Fish comes last.	Aquarius, Pisces

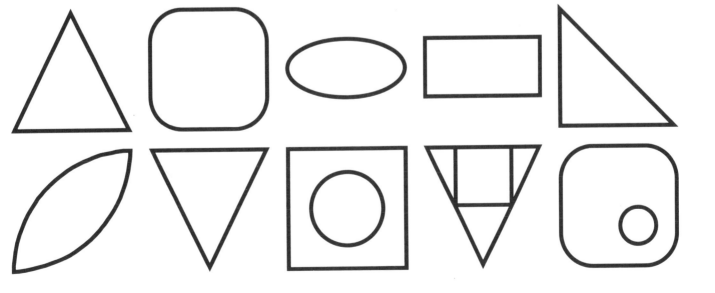

No

Warm-up

- As a whole class, ask students to define the word 'no'. Is 'yes' basically just the opposite of 'no', i.e. can you merely substitute 'yes' for 'no' and get the opposite meaning? A few examples should prove that you can't (e.g. you can't transform 'There's no bread' into 'There's yes bread' – 'some bread' would be OK. 'There's no point in going' could be converted into 'It might be a good idea to go' and certainly not 'There's yes point'!). Any student who comes up with a definition of 'yes' being the opposite should be asked to prove their point. Subject any other definitions to the same scrutiny.

- Ask students to think of any other ways to say 'no' in conversational English (e.g. yep/nope, yeah/nah, aye, etc.). Are 'yes' and 'no' adequate, do we need a 'yo' or a 'nis'? Then brainstorm students on expressions containing 'no' (e.g. by no means; no doubt you ...; make no bones about it).

(i) 'No' was originally used before consonants (e.g. no bread), as it was a reduced form of 'nan' or 'non' (which then gave us 'none'). 'No' is used in various contexts, some of which are listed here. It indicates objection, opposition or denial of something (No, I'm not going to do my homework.); it denotes the absence of something (but there are some exceptions: 'it was no distance' means that it wasn't very far, but the distance can still be measured); when qualifying a noun it suggests impossibility (There was no going back.).

1 Rules

- Students look at the illustrations and answer question 1. Get class feedback before they answer the other questions.
- Students now look at the box, which shows a jumbled list of rules for various situations. In groups students decide what situations the rules refer to. If you wish you can give them the categories: school, religion, diets, parents' rules to their children, museums. Get class feedback and give them the answers (obviously some items can fit more than one category). In groups again, students discuss questions 2–6.

➤○ *diet: j, p; family: a, c, l, n, s; religion (from the Books of Exodus and Leviticus in the Old Testament): d, e, i, k, o, q, r, u; school: b, f, g, h, m, t.*

Listening

- Students hear some odd school rules and other facts about a British preparatory school. First explain that a prep school is (generally) for boys, aged 8–13, who spend most of their year in a school away from their parents. This means they eat, sleep, study and play at the school, which charges a considerable amount of money to educate wealthy middle / upper-middle class children. Such schools used to be run on very military lines. Get students to imagine that they are going to ask someone who's been to a prep school some questions on the rules and life of the school. Write the questions on the board, giving suggestions where necessary so that you cover most of the speaker's answers. Students' task is to see which of their questions are answered.

1 Incredibly early – I mean I remember in my first year, so I would have been eight at the time, we had to be in bed by 7.30. By the time I left, when I was 13, I think we were going to bed at around nine. And then you weren't supposed to talk after lights out, if you got caught you were punished, given a good beating.

2 You weren't allowed to talk to anyone older than you unless they spoke to you first. And in any case you weren't allowed to use first names with anyone. I remember that if two or three people had the same surname, like Smith for instance, then they'd be known as Smith 1, Smith 2, Smith 3 etc., just like a prison.

3 We wore black, black jackets, black trousers, black ties, shoes everything apart from a black shirt. And this was all supposed to be in mourning for Queen Victoria. And you weren't allowed to deviate at all. I remember I once got my Mum to sew gold buttons on my jacket, and I think within half an hour of getting back to school they'd already been removed. The only thing they did let you do was to vary the thickness of your tie.

4 It was really revolting, I mean almost inedible. You were supposed to eat everything you were given, you couldn't leave anything on your plate, but it was so bad that I used to take a plastic bag in with me and fill it with the things I couldn't manage to eat, which was pretty much everything.

5 Not more than once a month, it was almost like having visiting hours in a prison. And when you first arrive it's terrible because you're used to seeing your parents every day before that. And the incredible thing was that they wouldn't let you write what you wanted to in your letters home, they'd actually censor your letters. So if you wrote 'Dear Mummy and Daddy I really miss you. I want to come home', they'd change it into 'I'm enjoying school so much that I hardly ever even have time to think about you.'

6 You weren't supposed to have any money at all. Not that it would have been much use, as you weren't allowed out into the village to buy anything anyway.

7 I suppose the rules that strike most people as being odd were things like that the fact that you weren't allowed to use umbrellas, you couldn't have a tape recorder until you'd been at the school three years, you couldn't phone your parents, and you weren't allowed to speak to the local children, and the fact that the older boys had the right to punish the younger boys, physically too.

Writing

- Students do one of the following tasks: (a) Students write rules to a particular game they like. They read out the rules and other students have to guess what game it refers to. (b) Write an essay outlining on what occasions our freedom needs to be curbed by rules. (c) Write some rules for life for a martian who has decided to emigrate to Earth. (d) Rules are made to be broken. Discuss.

1 Rules

 a

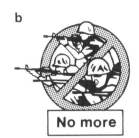 b **No more**

 c

 d

 e

 f

 g

 h **No sex please, we're British**

 i

 j **No comment**

1 Where might you find these signs? Who wrote them and why?

2 Which ones express rules? What would be the consequences of ignoring the rules?

3 Do we need rules? What happens to children (and adults in general) if you don't give them rules?

4 What's the difference between a good rule and a bad rule?

5 Is it sometimes right to break rules? What rules have you ever broken?

6 What should we do with people who break the rules?

a Do not accept lifts from strangers.

b Do not call out, unless asked to.

c Do not come home after midnight.

d Do not cook a young sheep or goat in its mother's milk.

e Do not cross-breed domestic animals.

f Do not distract or annoy others.

g Do not drop any litter.

h Do not eat, drink or chew.

i Do not follow the majority when they do wrong.

j Do not have snacks between meals.

k Do not hold back the wages of someone you have hired, not even for one night.

l Do not leave the lights on when you are not in the room.

m Do not leave the room until you are told to.

n Do not leave your clothes lying around.

o Do not mistreat a foreigner.

p Do not mix carbohydrates with proteins.

q Do not spread false rumours, and do not help a guilty man by giving false testimony.

r Do not steal or cheat or lie.

s Do not talk with your mouth full.

t Do not use walkmans, or radios or read magazines.

u Do not work on the Sabbath (i.e. Sundays or Saturdays for Jewish people).

2 Antonyms

- Students try to find **one word** antonyms for the words listed. Most of the words were obviously chosen to get students discussing whether the words actually have opposites or not. Where students can't find a one-word equivalent, they should discuss why it's not possible. In some cases, there may even be discussion of what the word means or whether it's a noun, a verb or adjective (e.g. book, dream, fear, fire, man, present). Thus, make sure students analyse the words in all their possible meanings (e.g. 'off' could be 'on' if you're talking about the TV, but 'OK' or 'fresh' if you're talking about milk).

3 No way

- Students read the items on the list and tick the ones that there is no way that they would consider doing. They then discuss these with their partner (you might need to pre-teach inversions, i.e. 'No way would I ever accept a bribe'; 'Nothing would ever make me drink alcohol', etc.).
- This is actually rather a tame exercise which could certainly be livened up either by you inserting some more interesting items onto the list, or simply by getting students to come up with their own lists to ask each other (but go round checking their lists for any items which may be too taboo for that particular class).

4 Nonsense?

- NB This is the kind of exercise that really needs to be adapted to suit your own taste. Although these proverbs were initially chosen because they all contain negatives (i.e. to be in theme with the rest of the unit), my students found them very provocative but this doesn't mean yours will. So, as with the rest of this book, feel free to replace all or some of them with your own favourite proverbs, quotations or whatever.
- Get students to look at the proverbs and sayings, some of which at first sight (and second too!) may appear to have no sense. The students' task is to paraphrase all of them (most paraphrases could begin with 'if'). Even if students don't understand the meaning, they should attempt to rewrite them. In pairs, students then compare their interpretations. Finally, get class feedback and give them the answers. Find out if students have equivalents to these proverbs in their own language.

🔑 *Most of the proverbs are fairly self explanatory. Here are explanations for some that may be difficult. 'No hate ...' means that if you are incapable of feeling hate then you won't be able to feel love either. 'Nothing question ...' if you don't doubt and question things, then you will never truly learn. 'The apple never falls ...' concerns heredity, i.e. that we are basically the same as our parents; 'You can't have your cake ...' means you can't have things both ways.*

Follow-up

- In a multilingual class, get each student to write down three or four popular proverbs from their country and to translate them into English. They should then read them out to their group who have to understand the meaning, discuss it and say whether they have equivalents in their own language.

Writing

- Virtually any of the proverbs on student's page could be set as an essay title for homework.

2 Antonyms

book	fear	learn	one	straight
dream	fire	man	present	think
earth	good	off	serious	white

3 No way

accept a bribe
go parachuting
break a tradition
go to a casino
build a house by yourself (or with friends)
have a champagne bath
change jobs/school
invite the teacher to your house
contradict the teacher/your parents
join the army or the police force
cry in public

learn a martial art
do yoga or other types of meditation
live permanently in another country
drink alcohol
sacrifice your own life for your country
go on a diet
steal something
go on holiday alone
tease or make fun of someone
go on strike

4 Nonsense?

Better the devil you know than the devil you don't.

Better to have been an old has been than a never was.

Nothing is impossible.

No pleasure without pain.

Nᴏ hate, nᴏ love.

You can't have your cake and eat it.

No one is indispensable.

No news is good news.

Nothing question, nothing learn.

Nothing comes of Nothing.

The apple never falls far from the tree.

Opinions

Warm-up

- Brainstorm students on what opinions have changed over the centuries and also in the recent past. Put the following prompts on the board: beauty, marriage, education, tastes, manners etc. Do they think that any of the fixed ideas we have now will change in the future – is it right (or normal) to assume that everything we think now is bound to be right and what previous generations thought is bound to be wrong? There could be enough material here to keep you going for several weeks, so keep the discussion brief if you have other plans in mind.

1 When I want your opinion, I'll give it to you

- Brainstorm students on meaning of quotation (i.e. I'm only interested in what I think, and you have to think like I think).
- Students then answer questions alone, and discuss their answers in groups. NB They can give more than one answer except for the first two questions.

Listening

- Students hear five people's opinions in answer to the question: 'In a relationship is it OK for you to have different opinions and beliefs from the other person?'. Copy the table in the key on to the board (without the answers!). Students should write Y, N or ? where appropriate.

🔑 (There might be some argument over the answers in the key.)

	1	2	3	4	5
OK to have different beliefs/values:					
a) as friend	?	Y	Y	?	Y
b) as lover	Y	N	Y	N	?
OK to have different interests:					
a) as friend	?	Y	Y	Y	Y
b) as lover	Y	N	Y	Y	?

1 I mean it really depends on how far you expect the relationship to go on for. If it's not going to be anything permanent then I don't see that it matters, in actual fact it's probably far more stimulating that way.

2 OK for friends, but I think in a love relationship there need to be some fundamental things you need to agree on. I could never go out with someone who had a different political outlook for example or who had different musical tastes for that matter.

3 Yeah, why not? I see a relationship, any kind of relationship whether it be with friends or in a stable love relationship, as being a constant learning process. And this process requires some kind of conflict. Now this doesn't mean that I'm advocating a total atheist going out with someone fanatically religious, but it does mean that there needs to be some kind of tension, some knowledge that you don't always know where it is that you're

going with each other, and while this tension can be kindled by love, it is only really fed by having differences of opinion and respecting those differences.

4 Not a good idea. Relationships only work where you know where you stand in some basic situations. I could never go out with anybody who didn't have a fundamental respect for family values. Nor could I stand someone with extreme political ideas. That's not to say that you can't have different interests, you may like football, I might hate it, that doesn't matter, in fact it would be really boring if we both always did the same things and thought the same things. But you do need to share some basic values.

5 I've got friends whose opinions I share and friends whose opinions I quite frankly detest. I've had love relationships with girls who shared my fundamental beliefs, and with girls who were on a totally different wave length. And they all ended in tears. Conclusion? I'm not made for relationships. No seriously, I certainly don't think it matters with friends, and with lovers; I just think there has to be something magical, something inexplicable, something almost spiritual but physical too, that has to click. And I'm still waiting.

Follow-up

- Students discuss which of the five opinions they agree with most – do they think there should be an element of conflict and magic in a relationship?

2 How liberal are you?

💣 Some students may find this exercise sensitive; in any case you can adapt the style of the exercise to topical subjects that your particular students would find interesting.

- Tell students that the statements refer to some arguments for and against three of the following topics: anarchism, animal rights, birth control, euthanasia, forced sterilisation of the unfit, state-registered brothels and surrogate mothers. They are to decide which argument refers to which topic, and whether the arguments are pro or con. Students then discuss the three subjects further, adding any more pros and cons they can think of.

🔑 *The three subjects are birth control (A), forced sterilisation (B) and euthanasia (C).*
1 *A pro* 2 *B pro* 3 *B con* 4 *C pro* 5 *B pro* 6 *A con*
7 *C con* 8 *C con* 9 *A con* 10 *A con*

Useful further reading:
M. D. Jacobson: *Pros and cons.*

Follow-up

- Students work in pairs and choose one of the other arguments (or any others you choose), and decide what their opinion is. S1 then imagines they were someone who held the opposite opinion (i.e. devil's advocate) and has to convince S2 of this opinion.

Opinions

1 When I want your opinion, I'll give it to you

1 Who has the most influence on your opinion? (Choose one only.)

   a friends
   b family
   c school teacher
   d religious teacher
   e mass media

2 At what age is it easiest to influence or change someone's opinion? (Choose one only)

   a 5–13
   b 13–18
   c 18–25
   d 25–40
   e 40+

3 Whose opinions would you never question?

   a parents
   b school teacher
   c religious teacher
   d government

4 In a friendship, is it important to have …?

   a pretty much the same opinions about politics
   b the same fundamental religious beliefs
   c the same interests

5 In a love relationship, should you have …?

   a pretty much the same opinions about politics
   b the same fundamental religious beliefs
   c the same interests

6 In life in general, is it better …?

   a to have the same opinions as the majority
   b not to force other people to have the same opinion as you
   c not to use power and fame to influence others
   d to invent an opinion rather than not have one at all

trust me, let go of the rope!

2 How liberal are you?

1 The problem is not whether X should be allowed but whether it should be compulsory or not. If something is not done soon, the world's resources will run out.

2 There is conclusive evidence that certain types of deficiencies and defects are hereditary, X would thus help to eradicate such diseases.

3 The administration of X would be very much open to abuse. It would always be used against the poor and never against the rich.

4 We put animals 'out of their misery', rather than let them suffer intolerable pain.

5 The production of the occasional genius is not sufficient compensation for the harm done and suffered by an increasing number of defectives in the community.

6 To suggest that X gives women more freedom to widen their horizons, socially or intellectually, just isn't true.

7 A request for X may only be due to a temporary feeling of despondency.

8 Legalised X would be a ready-made weapon for unscrupulous relatives which no amount of legal precautions could entirely guard against.

9 X is too often used to avoid imagined risks for purely selfish motivations. It is a denial of natural functions.

10 The almost unrestricted availability of X devices is encouraging immorality in the young and already leading them to reject the concepts of a society founded on the family.

3 Which is worse?

• In groups. Encourage students to use all kinds of comparative structures (as ... as, nothing like as, far more, etc.) rather than just 'worse than'.

Writing

• Students choose one of the six subjects and write a composition comparing the four elements.

4 Opinion polls

• Give students the survey (but **don't** tell them it came from *Cosmopolitan*), and tell them to follow the instructions, i.e. read, then discuss in groups.
• In addition, you could allocate one member of each group as a pollster. Then get feedback from each pollster, collate the results, and compare them with the *Cosmopolitan* results. You can then draw conclusions on what kind of class you are.

🔑 **1** *only females, see questions 2 and 8* **2** *Yes, in fact they surveyed 714 female students, and originally published the answers to 58 questions.* **3** *Their conclusion was: This generation is liberalish but personally ambitious rather than broadly idealistic.*

Follow-up

• Ask students to prepare a short survey on petrol and parking problems. Get them to start in pairs, then in groups of four, finally in groups of eight. Each group then selects eight questions. Groups then poll each other, and prepare short reports on the results. Now proceed to the listening.

Listening

• See **Follow-up** before doing the listening. Students hear a discussion around a survey on petrol and parking problems. Afterwards they can continue the discussion in their groups.

Questions: **1** What doesn't the first speaker understand about the percentage results in polls? **2** What were the three percentage results and what were they related to? **3** Summarise the ideas of the second person in relation to parking, petrol and transport.

🔑 **1** *Why only a relatively small percentage of people think that petrol prices and parking charges are too high.* **2** *Petrol 70%, reduced traffic 60%, car park charges 65%.* **3** *Basically to discourage people from using petrol by doubling its price and making inner city parking prohibitive. This can be done by resorting to trains both for personal and goods transport.*

A Do you know the thing that's always struck me as odd about opinion polls?

B What's that?

A The percentages. Like recently there was a survey about what people thought about traffic, and petrol prices, and public car parks, I mean the charges, for instance in some car parks now it costs something like £5 for half an hour.

B Yeah, but I don't see what you're getting at.

A What I mean is the percentages in the results. So there might be 70% of people who complained about high petrol prices, and 60% who want to see the traffic reduced, and 65% who think car park charges are too high. Well so does that mean that there are 35% who actually think the charges are OK and would even be prepared to pay more, and another 30% who think petrol prices are OK? I mean that's absurd, I don't know anyone who doesn't think they're not too high.

B Well actually I think we should pay more.

A Come on, you're joking.

B No seriously, more for petrol, even twice as much maybe, and certainly far more for inner city car parks.

A But why?

B More taxes on petrol to discourage people from using cars, and a kind of graded charging system for car parks depending on how far they are from the city centre.

A What do you mean?

B Well, if you park your car quite far from the centre then you pay a minimal amount as a kind of reward for not polluting the centre, then the further you get nearer the centre then the more you are penalised. Prices in the centre should be totally prohibitive. I mean with an efficient bus or tram service there's no excuse for using cars.

A Yeah, but you can't penalise people who don't use their car to go in town, I mean if you doubled the price of petrol it would cost you a fortune to go anywhere, even on short trips, and especially on holidays.

B Don't use your car then. Use a train.

A But what about lorries, I mean they use a lot of petrol to transport goods from one place to another.

B So what's to stop these goods being transported by train or even via canal?

A Well anyway, I still can't believe that 30% of those people who said car park charges were OK all think the same as you.

B Well, maybe that's where you are wrong. Just think about what I've said and you'll realise that perhaps it's not so stupid as it sounds.

3 Which is worse?

1 A writer earning $1m a week
A football player earning $1m a week.
A film star earning $1m a week.
A business man earning $1m a week.

2 Pouring toxic chemicals into a river.
Segregating blacks from whites.
Building nuclear power stations.
Selling arms to dictators.

3 Drinking over the limit and then driving.
Smoking in a non-smoking department.
Dropping litter in a park.
Spitting on the pavement.

4 Growing old.
Growing ugly.
Going senile.
Growing intolerant.

5 Losing your health.
Losing all your money.
Losing your religion.
Losing your reputation.

4 Opinion polls

Read this opinion poll and its results. Answer any
questions you can and then discuss them.

**1 Do you think your college years will be the best years of
your life?**
yes 49%   no 49%

2 Would you rather work for a man or a woman?
man 40%   woman 38%

**3 Do you think you are more knowledgeable about life than
your parents were at your age?**
yes 67%   no 10%   same 22%

**4 Do you think this country is a better place to live in than it
was 10 years ago?**
yes 24%   no 44%   same 31%

5 Which would you rather your fairy godmother gave you?
outstanding personality   61%
outstanding beauty   19%
outstanding intellect   19%

6 If you won £10,000 would you ...?
spend it all on travelling   63%
use it as a deposit on a house   17%
invest it in stocks and shares   14%
give it to family/friends/charity 7%

**7 If you could see your finals papers a week before the
exams, and get away with it, would you do it?**
yes 59%   no 40%

**8 Have you ever pretended to be less intelligent than you
really are in a man's company?**
yes 40%   no 59%

**9 Would your parents approve of you going out with
someone of a different race?**
yes 25%   no 29%   indifferent 46%

10 Do you vote the same way as your parents?
yes 42%   no 39%   don't know 18%

**11 If you could make £60,000 a year as any of the following,
which would you be a ...?**
journalist 34%   teacher 27%   doctor 15%
lawyer 12%   banker 7%   politician 6%

12 Which would you rather receive?
£10 million 53%   a Nobel prize 28%
a proposal of marriage 10%   an Oscar 9%

13 Would you change your religion for love?
yes 27%   no 69%

Now decide if the following statements are true or false.
Justify your choices.

1 This survey was directed at males and females.

2 The age of those being surveyed was probably between
18 and 23.

3 The results of the survey prove that the interviewees are:
(a) rebellious, politically fervent and altruistic.
(b) personally ambitious and quite liberal.

Personality

Warm-ups

- In groups of four, students write down whether they think the other three members are predominantly governed by their heart, head or wallet. They then discuss their ideas.

- In a class that knows each other well, put students in groups of four. Dictate the list below adding or deleting elements as you think fit. Students write down which member of the class they think: is best at English, is the most eccentric, is most likely to make a lot of money, has the most expressive face, would make the best prime minister, the teacher likes the most, was naughtiest as a child, etc. They then discuss their ideas.

1   Personality traits

- Students classify the adjectives into those with positive connotations (+), neutral (=), and negative (-). They then compare their answers in groups, and should also decide when certain normally unpleasant characteristics may be acceptable in certain circumstances, e.g. aggression (when a police officer shoots a terrorist?), being cruel to be kind (when someone tells a bad actor that they will never make Hollywood?). They should then try to identify the differences between related concepts, for example: ambition/competition, logic/rationality.
- With students who are more willing to talk about personal issues, get them to rate themselves from one to three (e.g. 1 not aggressive, 3 very aggressive). In pairs they either compare and discuss their own characteristics, or decide which five characteristics they'd look for most in a friend.
- An alternative, less personal, approach is to give students a list of jobs (comedian, dictator, police officer, Pope, stuntman/woman, etc.) and to decide which positive and negative traits are typically associated with such jobs.

Writing

- Students discuss one of these three titles: (a) 'Personality is not a result of genes and inheritance, but of our social environment.' (b) 'Every person has the defects of their qualities.' (c) 'It is harder to change human nature than change rivers and mountains.'

2   Fame

- Explain that a 'personality' is also another word for a celebrity or famous person. Before students read text, in groups they discuss well-known personalities in their country or in the world in general and work out what such people have in common (including what kind of personality, in the other sense, these people have).
- Students now read the text, then ask them where it may have come from – the kind of language should give some clues to the fact that it is from an interview (with Bob Dylan). Tell students that all the quotes come from a music magazine's interviews with various musicians. The musicians were all answering the same question; students should try and work out what the question was and then try to understand exactly what the musicians meant.

The question was: 'What is the greatest myth about fame?'.

(1) Tori Amos (2) Mark Pellow (3) Alison Moyet (4) Roland Orzabal (with reference to BandAid type concerts) (5) Jackson Browne (6) Shaking Stevens (7) Ice T (8) Paul Weller (9) Sinéad O'Connor (10) Peter Gabriel (i.e. gaps in your life or personality perhaps) (11) Lemmy (12) Chrissie Hynde (13) Billy Bragg

Follow-up

- Brainstorm students on the pros and cons of being famous, e.g. being instantly recognisable, being hounded by the press, never knowing whether people like you for who you really are or only because you're rich and famous. Finally get them to decide whether the negative things outweigh the positive ones.

Role-play

- One member of a group of four to six students chooses a famous personality that he/she would like to be (alternatively, you can choose someone for them, e.g. a member of the royal family, a prime minister or president, a film or music star; the person needn't necessarily be alive). The other students imagine that they are at a press conference interviewing this VIP. Give the interviewers a few minutes to prepare a few questions and the interviewee to reflect over answers to possible questions.

Writing

- Students choose one of these options: (a) Conduct a written interview (either in direct or indirect speech) with one or both of the following people: the partner of a famous person, the child of a famous person. The idea is to understand what it's like to live in someone's shadow. (b) Write a fan letter to your favourite pop or sports star.

1 Personality traits

aggressive	confident	dependable	imaginative	modest	prejudiced	sincere	understanding
ambitious	conscientious	discerning	impulsive	nervous	rational	snobbish	unpredictable
broad-minded	creative	generous	logical	observant	reckless	stubborn	vain
competitive	cruel	idealistic	materialistic	pessimistic	servile	tactful	wise

2 Fame

People treat people all the same.

It doesn't matter what the person's famous for, you could be famous for the shooting of the President or something, you're still famous and they put your picture on all the newspapers. You could be a famous fashion designer, or a famous movie star or a famous Wall Street executive, but you're still on your degree of fame. Everybody copes with fame in a different way, but nobody really seems to think it's what they went after. A lot of people go after fame and money, but they're really after the money, they don't want the fame. It's like, say, you're passing a little pub or an inn, and you look through the window and you see all the people eating and talking and carrying on, you can watch outside the window and you can see them all being very real with each other. As real as they're gonna be, because when you walk into the room it's over. You won't see them being real any more.

1 That it's gonna take away the pain.

2 That you feel famous. You don't.

3 That it justifies any means.

4 That it can close the hole in the ozone layer, feed the starving and find a cure for AIDS.

6 They say money doesn't bring happiness, it's a lie.

7 That everyone famous is rich.

9 That it makes you happy.

10 That it fills holes.

11 That it's important. That it somehow makes you feel cleverer or better than before.

5 That it's not any fun. It'll get you a good table in a restaurant. You can travel to places and gain entrance into places that might take you years to get into otherwise. That's a great privilege.

8 That it makes you somehow special.

12 That famous people are more interesting than ordinary people.

13 That it makes you omnipotent. It doesn't. It just allows you to magnify your worst characteristics so that you feel that you can get away with anything.

Personality

3 PsychoDraw

- Before students look at their page, ask them to draw a tree with a pen – very quickly, nothing elaborate and no crossings out.

Listening

- Now tell them that this is a psychological game and that they're going to learn how to interpret each other's trees. Get them to look at their page. The speaker describes how to interpret the various parts of the trees illustrated on their page, starting from the roots. At the first listening, the students' task is to note down in what order the speaker describes the pictures in each group (e.g. with reference to roots, the speaker describes thick, then thin and then no roots). Secondly, students note down what the speaker says about the various parts so that they can then use this information to interpret their pictures. The fifth extract relates to how to assess someone's imagination. With lower levels, you can skip the listening and just outline the interpretation yourself.

🔊 **1** *a, c, b* **2** *e, d, f* **3** *j, g, i, h* **4** *l, k, n, m*

📼 1 The tree represents intelligence and imagination. Basically there are four things to look for: the roots, the trunk, the branches and the foliage or fruit. The roots tell you literally how well grounded your intelligence is, so if you've drawn thick strong roots, then you've got a solid base to your intelligence and you're likely to be resolute in your decisions, you've got your feet on the ground so to speak. Thin straggly roots indicate a less well founded intelligence, but even if you've got no roots at all, this doesn't mean you've got no intelligence though it may mean that you don't look much beneath the surface, that you're not very analytical.

2 The trunk represents the amount of intelligence, but remember to look at the trunk in proportion to the other parts of the tree. For example, a thick trunk with little foliage or fruit on top, means a potentially high level of intelligence which isn't being exploited. In fact, it's far better to have a thin trunk with a mass of foliage on top, which shows that you use your intelligence to the full. If your trunk kind of bends to one side, it probably means that you were pressurised into following a particular direction in your life that you didn't want to.

3 The branches tell you what direction your intelligence is taking you. If some branches have been cut off, it could either mean that you decided to change direction yourself, or that someone literally cut your way and made you do things against your will. A lot of branches indicates a lack of direction and vision, whereas two or three branches means that you leave your options open to follow more than one career path. No branches may mean that you've channelled all your energy and intelligence into one area, you may be rather narrow minded as a consequence.

4 But the really important thing is the foliage and fruit; in proportion to the trunk, the more you have the better. Someone who draws a lot of individual pieces of fruit, is probably someone who is successful in all the various things they have to do at school or work or whatever. A mass of unclearly defined foliage may mean unfocused intelligence. No leaves, even if you do the drawing in winter, means that you're not exploiting your intelligence at all. The best thing is to have a balance of a few clearly defined branches with a good amount of leaves.

5 Your imagination can be seen from what kind of tree you draw and how original your tree looks. If, for example, the foliage on your tree looks like a cloud, it means that your imagination hasn't developed much since you were a child, as that's the kind of way children draw trees. If you draw a pine tree and you live in a country where pines abound, then you're lacking in both imagination and an ability to see outside your local reality.

4 Psychological tests

- Tell students that the questions were originally part of a personality test called 'Do you have social empathy?' Social empathy is the ability to re-live the experiences of others or, in other words, the ability to feel for oneself the emotions, moods and thoughts of another human being.
- Students read all the items, mark their answers and then discuss their answers in their group. Each group has to reach a decision on which is the best answer.
- Now give them the answers.

🔊 **1***a* **2***b* **3***a* **4***a*

Follow-up

- Tell students that the questions are based on some true social psychology studies. Get students to think about why some of the studies were conducted in the first place and what the implications of the findings are.

3 PsychoDraw

1

2

3

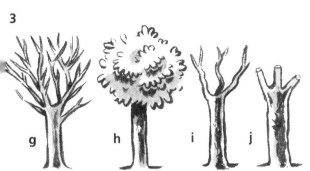

4

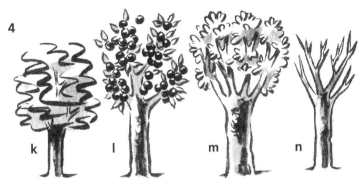

4 Psychological tests

1   An American research team played tapes which relayed identically worded information. The speaker was introduced as (a) a professor, (b) a member of the public, and (c) a delinquent. Who was best able to influence the listeners and bring about a change of attitude?
   a   the professor
   b   the member of the public
   c   the delinquent

2   A team of English psychologists gave a group of teenagers information to the effect that in ten minutes' time they would hear a lecture on 'Why teenagers should not be allowed to drive cars'. A second group received no information before the lecture. Which group of teenagers was more strongly influenced by the lecture?
   a   Teenagers who received the information before the lecture.
   b   Teenagers who received no information before the lecture.
   c   Both groups were equally strongly influenced.

3   Subjects were meant to find out whether a liquid tasted bitter. Social scientists diluted water with a bitter constituent. To 70% of the population this solution conveys a bitter taste, while it is tasteless to 30%. A group of ten subjects was composed of nine 'non-tasters', and one person who experienced the bitter taste very strongly and unequivocally. When this person described this sensation, how will the other nine group members behave?
   a   His unshakeably firm conviction influences the 'non-tasters': at the second sip they suddenly discover a slight bitter taste.
   b   The nine persons are not influenced by the 'taster'.
   c   The 'taster' is influenced by the nine subjects, so that at the second sip he no longer notices the bitter taste.

4   The American social scientist Marple asked three groups of people to give their opinion as to the correctness of a number of statements. The groups consisted of school pupils, students, and adults (care was taken to ensure that all had the same level of education). Four weeks later, the statements were once more put before the same people. They were again asked for their opinion, but this time with the additional remark, 'The majority of the other group did not share your opinion'. What influence did this additional remark have?
   a   64% of pupils, 55% of students, and 40% of the adults now changed their minds.
   b   64% of the adults, 55% of students, and 40% of pupils now changed their minds.
   c   There was no difference between the groups.

Quizzes

(i) This unit is basically a set of fill in or emergency exercises, between which there is no logical connection.

1 Phone calls

- Tell students to look at the six designs and to complete them in whatever way they want, but quickly and without asking any questions.
- When they've finished, brainstorm them on what the purpose of the quiz might be. Some students should come up with 'phone calls', it is, after all, the title of the exercise. Get them to try and relate what they've done to phone calls. If you get no response tell them that the quiz was invented by British Telecom, who claim that 'research has shown that when it comes to making telephone calls, most of us have a certain style. This simple test will give you an indication of your telephone approach and shed a bit of light on what makes you tick.'
- Can students now see a connection? Not even if they imagine that they are psychologists? No? OK. Look at the bottom of page 75 for the solution, which students should now read. Can students now see the connection? If they can't, and there's no reason why they should be able to, then you could discuss the whole theory of psychological tests and whether actually they're just fun for the people who invent them.

Follow-up

- Talk about phoning in general. Do students like the phone? Would they like to have a video phone?

Writing

- Students discuss this topic: 'The telephone and the television have destroyed the art of writing.'

2 All mixed up

- Brainstorm students on whether they do psychological quizzes in magazines. Ask them whether it is possible to learn something constructive from such tests. Now proceed to the exercise.
- Tell students that in this exercise the 12 questions were part of four different quizzes (three questions for each quiz). First the students need to be clear about the titles of the quizzes. Brainstorm the class to imagine the kinds of questions which would be applicable for such titles. Then they have to read and answer the questions and in pairs decide which questions refer to which title (some questions may appear to overlap, but this should promote discussion). Next they decide how the questions should be answered to score full marks in that quiz (e.g. if you are ambitious you would answer 'no' to c, 'no' to d, and 'yes' to b). Finally they can discuss their own personal answers. You may decide to drop some of these stages.

🔑 **1***D* **2***C* **3***C* **4***C* **5***B* **6***A* **7***D* **8***D* **9***B* **10***B* **11***A* **12***A*

Follow-up

- Put students in groups of four. Give them the titles of other possible questionnaires: Are you a good friend? Are you an optimist? How much stress is there in your life? Will you live to be a hundred? Are you satisfied with your job? In pairs get them to invent two or three questions for three of the titles. They then read their questions to the other two members of their group who have to guess which questions refer to which titles. They should then answer each other's questions.

1 Phone calls

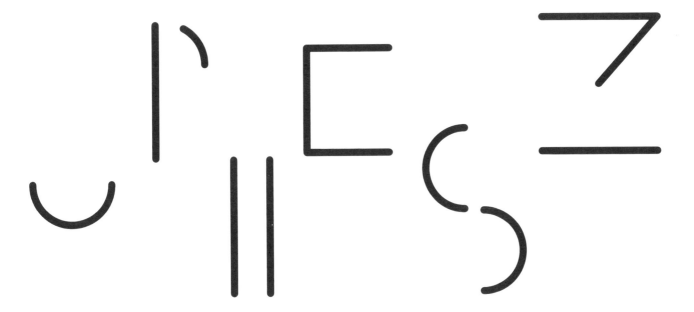

2 All mixed up

A Running your own life

C AMBITION

B *Health/Fitness*

D Sensation-Seeking

1 Do you find that people become boring when you can predict what they're going to say?

2 Do you try to do things immediately rather than put them off till later?

3 Do you let an escalator carry you along without walking yourself?

4 Do you find it difficult to concentrate on an important job when people around you are chatting?

5 Do you usually drink more than five cups of coffee a day?

6 Do you find it a waste of time planning ahead, because in the end something always turns up that causes you to change your plans?

7 Do you get restless if you are not involved in several different activities?

8 Are you turned off by people who say shocking things just to get a reaction?

9 Would you usually take the lift rather than the stairs to go up two floors?

10 Do you often fall asleep in front of the television?

11 **Do you make your own decisions regardless of what people say?**

12 Do you often feel that you are the victim of outside forces you cannot control?

Quizzes

3   General knowledge

- NB Before doing quiz, make sure you know the answers to questions **13**, **22** and **25**.
- Students do the quiz in groups. Make the exercise competitive by giving a prize to the group that answers the most questions in five minutes. Check answers.

1 *power/electricity measurements*   **2** *Mercury, Venus, Earth, Mars, Jupiter, Saturn, Uranus, Neptune, Pluto (in 1995 two new planets were discovered.)*   **3** *1914–18, 1939–1945 (though this will depend on when certain countries entered the war)*   **4** *Compact Disk, International Monetary Fund, Random Access Memory, Worldwide Fund for Nature*   **5** *e.g. UK, Belgium, Denmark, Netherlands, Spain etc.*   **6** *mile, litre*   **7** *Pacific*   **8** *Shakespeare*   **9** *elephant (660 days), cow (278), dolphin (360), human (267)*   **10** *economic group of European countries, Brussels*   **11** *iron, lead, silver, gold*   **12** *the British Prime Minister*   **13** *at time of writing Brazil*   **14** *black belt*   **15** *Argentinian dictator, died 1974*   **16** *French*   **17** *Japan*   **18** *ninth month of Muslim year, throughout which a strict fast is observed during hours of daylight*   **19** *USA, independence from Britain*   **20** *no, an arachnid, 8 legs (insects have 6)*   **21** *most famous pop group in the world, John Lennon*   **22** *?*   **23** *Britain*   **24** *English comic who became successful in Hollywood*   **25** *?*

Follow-up

In itself the quiz may not generate much talking. Below are some ways of promoting more discussion.

- Individually, students decide which are the three most and least important facts to know. They then justify their choices to the other members of their group. Then as a group they should formulate one common list. Get class feedback and see if whole class can reach a consensus.
- In groups, students categorise the questions into subject areas (which students themselves should decide). They then discuss what they consider to be the most important subjects to be knowledgeable about, decide whether they themselves are knowledgeable in these areas, and which areas they would like to be more knowledgeable in.

Writing

- It is better to know something about everything, than everything about something. Discuss.

4   Schedule P

- Another mystery quiz for students to find the meaning of! Tell students to complete the quiz individually. They must choose only one answer; they cannot write 'it depends'.
- Brainstorm students on the possible purpose of the test and who it is aimed at (age, sex, nationality, etc.). Now tell them that it is based on tests created by consultant psychologists to use at job interviews. Discuss with your students:
  1) what each question aims to discover about the candidate
  2) as prospective employers which statements they think would be the most suitable for a candidate to agree with
  3) the validity of such tests in job interviews

Follow up

- In groups, students discuss their answers to the questions. (With chatty groups this in itself could take up an entire lesson.)

3 General knowledge

1 What do amps, ohms, volts and watts have in common?

2 What are the names of the nine planets?

3 What were the dates of the first and second world wars?

4 What do CD, IMF, RAM and WWF stand for?

5 Name three countries which still have a royal family.

6 Which is longer and bigger – a mile or a kilometre, a pint or a litre?

7 Which is bigger – the Atlantic or the Pacific Ocean?

8 Who wrote Hamlet?

9 Which animal has the longest gestation period – cow, dolphin, human, elephant?

10 What is the European Union and where are its headquarters?

11 What are the names of these metals – Fe, Pb, Ag, Au?

12 Who lives at No. 10 Downing Street?

13 Which country has won the football World Cup the most times?

14 Who is the best at Judo – a white belt or a black belt?

15 Who was Juan Perón?

16 What European language is commonly spoken in Algeria?

17 Which of the following countries does not have the nuclear bomb – China, India, Japan, Pakistan?

18 What is Ramadan?

19 Who celebrates the fourth of July and why?

20 Is a spider an insect? How many legs do spiders have?

21 Who were the Beatles? Which member of the Beatles was shot and killed in New York?

22 Who is the President of the United States? And the Director General of the United Nations?

23 What country did Hong Kong formerly belong to?

24 Who was Charlie Chaplin?

25 How old is your English teacher?

4 Schedule P

Choose the statement you most agree with.

1 a My private life is my own affair.
  b I am happy to talk about my private life.

2 a Being criticised, both fairly and unfairly, is not a major problem for me.
  b I react badly to all kinds of criticism.

3 a I tend to be ruled by my heart.
  b My head is in control of what I do.

4 a If I see children throwing litter on the ground I intervene.
  b It's got nothing to do with me if other people's children throw litter.

5 a I prefer working alone.
  b I like doing project work with other people.

6 a I am good at telling jokes.
  b I prefer listening to jokes rather than telling them.

7 a I know where everything is on my desk.
  b I often accumulate piles of paper on my desk over several months.

8 a I prefer to lead than be led.
  b Responsibility worries me.

9 a Principles often get in the way.
  b There are some things that I would never do.

10 a I just love parties.
  b I tend to find a quiet corner to sit in when I'm at a party.

---

1 If you've drawn all letters or just one picture, then you're a VERBALISER. You prefer to think in words and approach problems in a more analytical way using the left, more objective side of the brain. The phone is your natural medium and you rarely find yourself tongue-tied or lost for words. But be careful not to miss the unspoken emotional messages conveyed by tone of voice and silence. Listen particularly carefully to any conversations in which feelings are more important than fact.

2 An equal number of letters and pictures means you're a WORD ARTIST — someone who's at much at home with words as with images. It suggests flexibility of thinking which can quickly adapt to the situation. When required you can adopt a logical objective approach to solving a problem. On other occasions you depend on intuition and hunches to come up with a solution. With an adaptable mind like yours, you'll be well suited to running your own business where intelligence and intuition both play an important role.

3 If you've drawn all pictures or just one letter, you can be described as a VISUALISER. Your thinking focuses on images rather than words which suggests you are better at using intuition than logic. The right hand side of your brain, which handles fantasy, imagination and creative thinking is dominant. The phone needs to be handled with care when you're forced to deal with facts and figures. Pay close attention and double check the details. But you have a natural advantage when dealing with a call which demands diplomacy and tact. You also have the upper hand in detecting the often hidden emotions underlying a telephone conversation.

Revolution

(i) The word 'revolution' has its roots in the Latin 'revolvere', meaning to revolve. This sense still remains – long playing records go round at 33 revolutions per minute (rpm). Two words previously used to describe our modern day idea of revolution are treason (i.e. betraying a lawful authority) and rebellion (from the Latin 'rebello' meaning to take up the fight again, bellum = war). The change in meaning from 'turning' to political rising is logical: a revolution is literally a turning over of the authority, a turning of the wheel of fortune. The revolution which led to the English Civil War was actually called a rebellion at the time, though the relatively minor events a few decades later in 1688 were known as the Glorious Revolution, and this was the beginning of the meaning which it has today. Interestingly, an uprising is still called a rebellion by the opposing party, when the latter party is still convinced that they still only have an insurrection on their hands. From the mid 18th century the words 'revolt' and 'revolting' began to acquire the meanings of disgust that they have today. The terms 'revolutionary' and 'revolutionise' (the latter was coined around the period of the French revolution) have now taken on a different meaning, via the industrial, sexual and technological revolutions, and are probably used more in the language of advertising than in politics, to mean 'innovative' and 'charismatic'.

Warm-up

- Students write down three words that they associate with the word 'revolution' and in groups discuss their ideas. Brainstorm students on the differences in meaning between 'revolution', 'revolt', 'rebellion' and 'coup'.

1 Talkin' 'bout a revolution

- Students identify which revolutions are depicted in the picture and discuss what they know about them.

🔊 **1 English:** *Parliament divided over Charles I's ideas on divine right of Kings. overspending, irresponsible amorous behaviour, dubious parliamentary dealings. Civil War ensues in 1642 and ends 1649; Royalist army defeated and Charles beheaded. Republic (the first in modern Europe?) under Cromwell ends with restoration of monarchy in 1660.* **2 American:** *1775, Lexington, first armed encounter between English and American troops. England had been sucking its American colony dry. George III declares the Americans rebels and War of Independence begins. On July 4 1776, thirteen states declare independence. Boston Tea Party follows. 1776–1783 England loses virtually all battles, Tory government falls. September 3 1783, the two sides sign a treaty which recognises the independence of the 13 states.* **3 French:** *Country in grave economic and social crisis. Royal family, nobility and clergy totally indifferent to needs of the people. Summer 1789, crowds of artisans, shopkeepers, labourers roaming towns in search of arms and demanding bread and liberty. July 14 1789, storming of the Bastille; August 4, Assembly abolishes feudal rights and privileges August 26, declaration of the rights of men and citizens.* **4 Russian:** *Usual story of monarchy's and nobility's indifference to peasants and workers. January 22 1905, Cossacks fire on demonstrators who are taking petition to Tsar Nicholas II. October general strike. December, St Petersburg general insurrection leads to Tsarist repression. March 1917, revolution begins; Tsar abdicates; family arrested; Lenin returns. October Revolution, Soviets gain power and the rest is history!*

- Students then discuss the questions, in groups. In multilingual classes, make sure there is the widest range of nationalities in each group, as this should lead to some interesting discussions.

Follow-up

- Students imagine they are going to overthrow their school (if they are still at school), or attack a neighbouring town or country. First they should decide why they want to rebel (or attack), what their grievances are, and their plan of action. Alternatively, if you are teaching in a state school, divide the class into groups of 'pupils' and groups of 'teachers', giving each group five or ten minutes to discuss and write down the grievances (pupils) or answers to anticipated grievances (teachers). Then put two pupils with two 'teachers' and let them argue it out!

2 The green revolution

- Students read texts and discuss questions in groups.

(i) The first passage is from a lecture, entitled 'The Future of England', given by John Ruskin in 1869 to members of the Royal Academy. Ruskin expressed his fears about a nation that he believed, as the result of mass industrialisation, would soon find itself infested with criminals, people who had been made out of work by machines. 'By hand labour, therefore, and by that alone, we are to till the ground'. Most modern machinery he referred to as kettles, 'smoking kettles' for ploughing, 'floating kettles' for going on the sea. He exhorted his listeners to 'open all the land, purifying your heaths and hills, and waters, and keeping them full of every kind of lovely natural organism, in tree, herb, and living creature. All land that is waste and ugly, you must redeem into ordered fruitfulness; all ruin, desolateness, imperfectness of hut or habitation, you must do away with.' Needless to say, no-one listened to a word he said! The second passage comes from a little book called *Go ahead and live* by Mildred Loomis published in 1965, though Mr Borsodi, a real visionary, it would seem, published his article in 1943.

Revolution

1 Talkin' 'bout a revolution

1 Has your country, in the last 100 years, witnessed any revolutions, rebellions or coups? If so, why did they take place? Who was fighting who, and what were the results?

2 Can blood and violence ever be justified in changing the status quo? What are the alternatives?

3 What things would you like to change in your country?

2 The green revolution

> We are not richer for the machine, we only employ it for our own amusement. For, observe, our gaining in riches depends on the men who are out of employment, consenting to be starved, or sent out of the country. But suppose they do not consent passively to be starved, but some of them become criminals, and have to be taken charge of and fed at a much greater cost than if they were at work, and others, paupers, rioters, and the like, then you attain the real outcome of modern wisdom and ingenuity.

> The first time the Green Revolution was used in print was in the Christian Century article by Ralph Borsodi. Here Mr Borsodi reported his findings from years of research: that home-production of food, clothing (and sometimes shelter) are more efficient than factory productions of these things; that modern, centralized, monopolized production creates international conflict and war. He urged scientists to develop technology suitable for home and small-scale production. This seems even more desirable as automation displaces more and more factory workers.

1 What do these two passages have in common? When do you think they were written?

2 Do you think that ever increasing technology is both dehumanising and endangering to peace in the world?

3 Do you prefer a centralised or decentralised system of government?

4 Do you agree with New Age-type philosophies of rediscovering what nature has to offer and becoming self sufficient? Would you like that kind of lifestyle?

Revolution

3 The women's revolution

- Students read the quiz, answer questions, and compare answers in groups of four (where possible, divide the sexes equally among the groups). This is obviously a particularly interesting exercise in multilingual groups with both sexes well represented. As an alternative: instead of reading the quiz, students can invent their own, then in groups of four collate their questions, and ask the same questions to another group.

Writing

- Students discuss this question: Is it better to be a man or a woman in your country?

(i) (1) In Britain only 7% of peers and 9.2% of MPs (1994 figures) are women. Women are excluded from parliament – directly from the House of Lords, by primogeniture (the exclusive right of the eldest son to inherit his father's estate), and indirectly from the House of Commons, by anti-social hours and lack of childcare. The legal system too, with the vast majority of judges being male, obviously favours men, this is especially true in rape cases. (5) Compare the meanings of 'spinster' and 'bachelor'. (7) The Bible has this to say about women: 'It is not good for the man to live alone. I will make a suitable companion to help him' (Genesis 2:18). After Eve had been caught eating the apple, God said to the woman 'I will increase your trouble in pregnancy and your pain in giving birth. In spite of this, you will still have desire for your husband, yet you will be subject to him' (Genesis 3:16). In St Paul's letter to Titus he wrote that older women 'must teach what is good, in order to train the younger women to love their husbands and children, to be self-controlled and pure, to be good housewives who submit themselves to their husbands' (Titus 2:5). See also 1 Peter 3:1–4. (8) The British government's

'Equality for Women' White Paper of 1974 said: '... the unequal status of women is wasteful of the talents of half our population in a society, which, more than ever before needs to mobilise the skill and ability of its citizens'. Twenty years later, a leaflet published by the Equal Opportunities Commission stated that: '... women still earn only 79% of men's full-time hourly earnings. They cluster in "women's jobs", often undervalued and underpaid. 76% of clerical and secretarial employees are women. Women are entitled to equal pay to men but if they do manage to take a case to court the average claim takes nearly three years.' (10) 48% of secondary school teachers in GB are women, but only 20% are head teachers; 70% of language students are women, 86% of engineering and technology students are men. Get students to discuss what subjects are typically chosen by girls, and which by boys, and what results this has.

The Equal Opportunities Commission is a good source for more information.

4 33 revolutions per minute

- Students read the text and answer questions. Obviously, if you can get hold of any of the records mentioned in the text and here below, then you'll add another dimension to the lesson.

(i) Possibly the most influential black singer, in terms of enlightening young people politically, was Bob Marley, who is also the most famous reggae singer. Another black singer, who became popular in the late 80s was the American singer, Tracy Chapman, who made a name for herself with a song entitled **Talkin' 'bout a revolution**, in which she predicted that those who were standing without hope in the unemployment lines would eventually rebel and try to get what was theirs.

3 The women's revolution

'... the first object of laudable ambition is to obtain a character as a human being, regardless of the distinction of sex.'

(A Vindication of the Rights of Women, 1792)

In your country...

1 Do women have the right to vote? When did they acquire this right? Are they well represented in parliament?

2 Do you have arranged marriages? Do women have any say in the arrangements?

3 Do women have to serve and obey their husbands?

4 Can men have more than one wife? Can women have more than one husband?

5 Are unmarried women and unmarried men considered in the same way?

6 Do women have to be accompanied when they leave the house? Why?

7 What role do women play in religious activities? Can women dress as they wish?

8 Are women allowed to do the same jobs as men? For the same salary?

9 Do teenage boys and girls have to be home at night at the same time? If not, why not?

10 Do girls and boys have the same educational opportunities in your country?

4 33 revolutions per minute

Modern music has always gone hand in hand with a spirit of rebellion and revolution. The Beatles were the first to entitle a song *Revolution* and each generation has their own music with which they identify and with which they criticise the generations before them. This is done initially in the style of the music itself; so punk with its loud, cacophonous and turbulent sound in short three minute bursts was in direct conflict with the so-called dinosaurs or establishment of rock who preceded them with their long grandiose almost orchestral pieces. But punk was of course aimed at questioning the capitalist authorities behind the mega-rock stars of the 60s and 70s. Punk faded quickly, and as in politics, the dinosaurs survived. Only black music has really retained any credibility in its revolutionary fight. Back in 1974, Gil Scott Heron, a pre-punk, pre-rap black poet wrote a song called *The revolution will not be televised*, in which he told his listeners that they would not be able stay at home and watch the revolution on TV, and then slip out for a couple of beers during the commercial break, nor would it make them look 2 kilos thinner and nor would NBC, the TV channel, be able to predict the result. What it would do would be to put them in the driving seat, and black people would be in the streets looking for a brighter day.

1 Do you associate yourself with the music of your generation? What values of the previous generation do you question?

2 Is music a valid means of promoting social and political change?

3 Is it a contradiction that famous musicians, who inevitably accumulate vast sums of money and live superstar lifestyles, talk about revolutionary behaviour?

4 Do you like rap music and reggae? Has it in anyway helped you to understand the position of black or fellow black people?

Science

Warm-ups

- Students discuss the question 'What is Science?' First brainstorm students on a list of scientific subjects. They then decide if they really are sciences or not. What about astrology (see **Zodiac: Space research**), graphology, medicine, philosophy, political sciences, psychology (see **Personality: PsychoDraw**), sociology, theology?

(i) The word 'science' derives from the Latin 'scientia' (knowledge) and one definition of science is 'knowledge acquired by study'. Another definition is that for something to be scientific one must be able to demonstrate it repeatedly, i.e. if an experiment cannot be repeated by other researchers in another place (reproducibility) then its results cannot be considered as scientific facts. Students can then discuss what we need science for and the role of science today.

- Brainstorm the class on the most important inventions and discoveries over history (e.g. the lever, fire, the wheel, America, the computer, the aeroplane, the origin of the species, penicillin, car, plane, electricity). In groups of six to eight, students should then prioritise them. One list should order them on the basis of how important they were in relation to the history of mankind and technological development (e.g. without the 'discovery' of the lever many other later developments would have been impossible). The second list should order them in terms of how difficult it would be to live without them now, e.g. fire until recently was an essential means for cooking, but we now have electric and microwave cookers. If there were no wheels what alternative means of transport could there be (mini rockets strapped to our backs)?

1 Science: the systematic observation of ...

- Precede this with the first warm-up. Dictate these nouns: colour, dream, horse, life, sky. Tell them to write two definitions for each of them, one as if for a child and the other for a dictionary of science and technology; tell them not to worry if they are unable to do all the definitions but that they must avoid using the key word itself in their definitions. This exercise could be set for homework at the end of the previous lesson.

- In pairs, S1 reads out a definition and S2 decides what word is being defined and who for. In groups, students then discuss definition writing, identifying which ones were the most difficult to define and why; were the scientific definitions more difficult than the children's ones or vice versa? Then get them to read the definitions on the student's page, firstly they should identify the ones that they themselves defined (and see how well their definitions match the 'official' ones) and then guess the subject of the other definitions. Finally they should rewrite the definitions of fear, human, language, telephone, and race as if for the children's dictionary.

➤O **1** *human* **2** *colour* **3** *life* **4** *dream* **5** *sky* **6** *fear*
7 *horse* **8** *language* **9** *telephone* **10** *race*

2 How things get invented

- Precede with the second warm-up. Tell students to look at the four illustrations above the text, which show a radar, ring structure of benzene, printing press, and a submarine. Make sure students understand what they are. Tell them to read the six paragraphs and to match the pictures with how they were invented. Two paragraphs will be left – students are to try and work out what inventions they refer to (i.e. zip and bra – the illustration at the bottom shows a corset, mentioned in the bra extract).

➤O **1** *printing press* **2** *radar* **3** *zip/zipper* **4** *bra* **5** *benzene*
6 *submarine*

(i) You can tell students some of the following useless but interesting facts. Biros were first publicised as high-altitude and underwater pens. Bakelite was first used for the gear knobs of Rolls Royces. The idea of chewing gum was an attempt to make a substitute for rubber. Edison (inventor of the light bulb) hid himself in a cupboard under the stairs when he wanted to solve a problem. Fritz Haber, the chemist who invented synthetic fertilisers, spent years trying to find a method to extract gold from seawater.

Further useful reading: Hunkin: *Almost everything there is to know.* (Hamlyn); Eureka: *An illustrated history of inventions.* Macualay: *The way things work.* (Dorling Kindersley)

1 Science: The systematic observation of ...

1 The group of mammals characterized by an erect stance, a large, highly developed brain, and the use of tools and language.

2 The sensation, determined by wavelength, that is generated by light in the visible spectrum.

3 The condition that distinguishes organisms such as humans, animals, and plants from organic matter and from dead organisms.

4 A mental phenomenon that occurs during sleep, in which a series of images, thoughts, and emotions resemble actual perceptions or events of the wakeful state.

5 The apparent flattened dome seen as extending above the earth.

6 A strong and unpleasant emotional state brought about by the threat of danger, pain, or suffering.

7 A mammal of the Equidae family, characterised by a slender neck and a graceful body with long legs, solid hooves, and a long neck covered with a mane; domesticated throughout the world.

8 The organised system of speech sounds that humans use to communicate with one another, or the written representation of these speech sounds.

9 A device that converts human speech into variations of electric current for the purpose of transmission.

10 An interbreeding subgroup of a species whose individuals are geographically, physiologically, or chromosomally distinct from other members of the species.

2 How things get invented

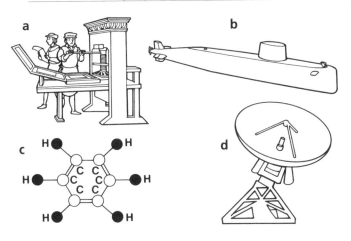

1 At a wine harvest festival the inventor noticed a wine press and saw it as a way to print evenly from hundreds of individual letters.

2 Developed from the bizarre suggestion of a radio death-ray for shooting down planes.

3 It was originally invented in 1891 as a way to do up boots, but was later exploited by the US Navy as a means to fasten up flying suits. An Austrian surgeon extended its use, when he sewed one into a man's stomach so that it was instantly accessible for internal dressings!

4 One night in 1914 before a party, a New York debutante, Caresse Colby with her French maid, who were both sick of wearing corsets (see below), devised the prototype from two pocket handkerchiefs, some pink ribbon, and thread. Friends liked it, and persuaded her to make ones for them too. When a total stranger wrote asking for a sample of her 'contraption', enclosing a dollar, she decided to exploit her invention.

5 The founder of organic chemistry apparently dreamed of a snake biting its tail and realised the ring structure of six carbon atoms in benzene.

6 This was invented by an Irish schoolmaster in New York, with the intention of sinking the British Navy.

corset

Science

3 The future?

- Tell students that a group of young children were asked to draw pictures of how they imagine things will be in one hundred years and what scientists will be able to do. Their page illustrates some of these children's pictures. The students' task is to work out what the child has tried to draw and what his/her reasoning might have been. Get class feedback and then give them the answers. In groups, students then choose one or two of the pictures and discuss the implications (some of these drawings reflect ideas which are already a reality).

a *mobile home* **b** *back-rocket (for personal transport)*
c *a tree which you can grow anything on* **d** *language glasses (for automatic translation)* **e** *square chickens (easier to slice and pack)*
f *love, dreams and brains bottles (for instant love, choose-your-own-dreams, extra intelligence)*

Writing
- Scientists should be free to carry out any experiments they like, regardless of utility, cost and ethics. Discuss.

Listening
- Students hear two people arguing about genetic engineering. Ask students to fill in a grid, marked pros and cons, then to continue the argument themselves.

pros	cons
– can produce more	– accidents with
– can produce fruit that doesn't	micro-organisms
rot and animals that eat less	– more dangerous than AIDS
– able to detect disease	– what use if there's
through genetic screening	no cure for the disease?
and therefore will prevent	– eugenics
diseases being passed on	– invasion of privacy
	– may affect chances
	of employment

A I've just been reading this amazing article about genetic engineering. The things they can do now.

B Yeah, it's frightening isn't it?

A Well, not a bit. I mean if we can produce fruit that doesn't rot, animals that eat less and produce more, what's so scary about that?

B OK. But you know those new micro-organisms that they are producing, (A: Yeah) well you only need a laboratory accident and the effects would be far more disastrous than AIDS for instance.

A Why are you always so negative? (B: I'm not negative.) Soon I'll be able to have a genetic screening done and they'll be able to tell me what diseases I'm likely to have.

B OK. But what if they tell you you're going to have a disease for which there's currently no known cure. That's not going to be much help is it?

A Yeah, but if I know it's hereditary then I might think twice before having any children.

B But you know where all this is leading don't you? To a revival of eugenics, like they're going to be able to remove potentially harmful genes, like the ones that cause criminality, low IQ.

A And people like you with a bit of luck!

B No seriously. They can take a piece of someone's hair now and tell you all about that person's medical life. Now that could be an incredible invasion of someone's privacy.

A How do you mean?

B Look. So at your job interview they ask you for a piece of hair, ring you up ten days later or whatever and tell you they don't want to employ you because you've got such and such a disease and you might die in five years.

A Don't be absurd. (B: I'm not being absurd.) Do you think people would let them get away with that, huh? What is all this? It sounds like you've been reading *1984*. Why don't you look on the practical side of things for a change?

B Practical?

4 Science fiction

- Brainstorm students on science fiction (often abbreviated to sci-fi) – what are its typical elements (e.g. location, appearance, food, habits)? Do they like it as a genre? Do they read/watch sci-fi books/films? What are the common criticisms of the genre? Many people associate sci-fi with robots, radar guns and star wars, but sci-fi is the perfect way to express philosophical ideas and possible future lifestyles, and to criticise current social and political attitudes.

- Tell students that the extracts about ways of living come from two completely different sources: one is a science fiction book, the other is from some anthropological notes on a record sleeve of some Indian music. Their task is to decide which extracts go with which sources.

1, 4, 7, and 8 refer to record sleeve notes to some music by a Bangladeshi tribe called the Garos. The rest refer to Ursula le Guin: The Dispossessed, a wonderful book containing a wealth of provocative ideas that can be converted into lessons.

I have no other information about the Garos. In *The Dispossessed* a group of people under their follower, Odo, leave an authoritarian hell-planet (earth) to form a new society on another planet which has very few resources. The people own nothing (hence the title), which extends to children being separated from parents soon after birth, and being given a unique name which indicates neither sex nor family (names are generated randomly by a computer). Men and women are equal, there is no religion (therefore impossible to blaspheme) and no taboos (hence no swear words). People move from job to job, but work in very harsh conditions imposed by their unfriendly environment.

82   Science

3 The future?

4 Science fiction

1 By law only women possess wealth. Men are allowed to administer the property but traditionally it cannot change hands without the consent of the women.

2 People's names give no indication of whether they are men or women.

3 Learning centres taught all the skills that prepare for the practice of art: training in singing, metrics, dance, the use of brush, chisel, knife, lathe and so on. It was all pragmatic: the children learned to see, speak, hear, move, handle. No distinction was drawn between the arts and the crafts; art was not considered as having a place in life, but as being a basic technique of life, like speech. Painting and sculpture served largely as elements of architecture and town planning.

4 People are divided into exogamous clans (i.e. they can only marry someone from another tribe) and marriage proposals come from the woman who may elope with her chosen man or send her relatives to capture him.

5 There are no locks on the doors of houses. No one has to do anything that they don't want to. 'Work' and 'play' are virtually synonymous.

6 Their language has no swear words or blasphemous expressions.

7 When somebody dies the body is washed, laid out in the house and kept there for two days before being burnt. During this period women keep watch over the body wailing unceasingly. These lamentations consist of recitation of the qualities and good deeds of the deceased.

8 Sacrifices are performed as a means of placating spirits that are supposed to be the cause of disease.

9 Their culture and ideas are based on the writings and sayings of a woman who escaped with her followers from an oppressive materialistic society.

10 Possessive pronouns are rarely used — instead of referring to 'my mother' most children say 'the mother', and rather than saying 'This one is mine and that's yours', they say 'I use this one and you use that'.

(i) The whole of this unit is designed to introduce students to this book and to the art of discussion in particular. The exercises are designed to be followed in sequence. Either begin directly with exercise 1 or use the first warm-up. Use **Taking turns** as a second warm-up, if this unit spreads over more than one lesson.

Warm-up

- Brainstorm students on why we need to talk (communicate; impart factual information; express opinions, thoughts, ideas; find out information; tell stories, jokes; etc.).

1 Madam I'm Adam

- The curious title to this exercise is supposedly Adam's first words to Eve when he introduces himself – it is, of course, really one of the most famous English palindromes (i.e. a sentence that you can read both forwards and backwards).
- If this is the group's first lesson together, you could get students to go round the class introducing themselves to each other. Then do the listening.

Listening

- Students hear two women (from Uganda and China) talking about how people are introduced in their countries. Their task is simply to listen for interest, then to read the passage, and then to answer the questions, using the listening and the passage as a stimulus.

1 Among the Acholi it's very impolite to introduce people in front of their faces. You wait until the guests are gone before you introduce them, you say this one who was sitting here is the son of so and so. And that comes partly because we sort of live in a huge community and everybody knows everybody else, so usually you know one another.

2 We introduce and we normally we inform the other about their job, their social position, which are the most important things. Guests are considered the most important person in a family, so if you don't have money, you have to borrow money to prepare a good dinner.

- Now tell them to read all the other four passages in the unit, but not to read the questions. Write the following instructions on the board: Find a passage: (a) about the history of discussion, (b) outlining a teacher's views on discussion in the country where he teaches, (c) from a teacher's manual on how to manage classroom discussions, (d) discussing rules of conversation.
- Check the answers and then move on to what you consider to be the most appropriate exercise.

➤ **a** *Devil's advocate* **b** *Toeing the line* **c** *Taking turns* **d** *Silence is golden*

2 Silence is golden

- Students read passage. Do questions 1 and 2 as a whole class activity. This is a golden opportunity to lay down some rules for group discussions: we've all had those students who just love to dominate discussions leaving everyone else either bored or angry; this is your chance to squash them in advance! (If students do insist on dominating the discussion, you should try and take them aside as soon as possible, for example at the end of the lesson, and gently help them to understand why their behaviour is unacceptable.) Students should come up with a variety of rules (many of which will probably be summarised in **Taking turns**). In discussions students should be encouraged to ask each other questions, listen carefully, not maliciously provoke or upset, and generally give each other space and show interest.
- Elicit as many phrases as possible for question 3, as these can then be learned and used during later discussions. You might also like to teach some other structures, e.g. what to say if you don't understand, how to clarify both what you're saying (what I mean is ..., what I'm trying to say is ...) and what the speaker is saying (so you mean that ..., so your point is that ...) etc.
- Students can discuss questions 4 and 5 in groups. In a multilingual class you should get some interesting viewpoints.

1 Madam I'm Adam

1 How do you introduce people in your language? And in English?

2 What do you talk about to people you've just met for the first time?

3 When you have nothing to say, is it always best to say nothing?

Not everyone feels that they have to introduce strangers to each other. Some American Indian and central African tribes have no formal rituals for helping people who meet for the first time to find out a few basic facts about each other – for example, their name and where they come from. There is no sense of having to speak as a form of politeness.

2 Silence is golden

1 What 'rules of conversation' can you think of?

2 What can you do if someone always wants to speak? How can you avoid yourself giving monologues?

3 What phrases do we use to break into a conversation?

4 What do you do if there is a silence in the conversation?

5 On what occasions is it best or right to remain silent?

There are even 'rules' about silence. It has been said that, in a conversation between two English speakers who are not close friends, a silence of longer than about four seconds is not allowed (which means that people become embarrassed if nothing is said after that time — they feel obliged to say something, even if it is only a remark about the weather). Many of the rules of conversation can in fact be broken, but notice that people usually acknowledge the fact if they do break them.

3 Toeing the line

- As this passage highlights, not all cultures place much importance on discussion. Your job is to convince such people that discussion is important, especially in terms of learning a language. Questions 2 and 3 are designed for non-western students. Question 5 is important as it should make students aware that it is their duty to try and involve the more reticent participants. Get students to be conscious that a good discussion depends as much on them as it does on the topic of discussion itself.

- (i) This piece comes from a reader's report on this book in which he explained the difficulties of using discussions in a country, Malaysia, where people are simply not used to discussing things and are quite happy to say 'yes', 'no' or whatever they think would follow the party line.

4 Devil's advocate

(i) Question 1 poses an interesting question. To discuss originally meant 'to strike asunder', 'to scatter'. It then came to mean to examine and investigate, and then to debate. One obsolete meaning was 'to settle or decide as a judge', which indicates how important it is that students reach some kind of conclusion. A conversation originally meant a 'frequent abode', then 'living together' and a place for having 'dealings with people', only much later did it come to mean an 'interchange of thoughts and ideas'. Today it basically means 'familiar talk' (Up until 1857 in legal language *crim. con.*, 'criminal conversation' meant adultery). The difference is thus quite clear: a discussion is something more formal and elevated, to air and weigh ideas, and then to reach a conclusion; a conversation is merely an exchange of ideas without any specific reasoning. Some people would say that you can have a discussion with a relative stranger, even someone you don't like; whereas a conversation is an altogether more intimate affair. Speaking and discussing are related in the same way as talking and conversing. To talk originally meant to chatter or to prattle (what a lovely word!), it has the same etymology as 'tale'. The *OED* gives one meaning as 'to speak emptily or trivially', 'to indulge in idle or censorious gossip'. Like conversation it is more informal (we can say an 'informal talk' but rarely an 'informal speech'). To speak comes from the Latin 'spargere' (to scatter words, thus a very similar root as discussion). It now means to 'express or communicate opinions'. It has a loftier edge than talk. Talk sounds like something naturally acquired (my child could already talk when he was two), whereas to speak is something more studious (we wouldn't say 'Can you talk English?', similarly you talk in your sleep, you don't speak).

5 Taking turns

- Students read the text and discuss question 1. You may like to do questions 2–5 as a whole class activity, as it is also important for you to express your own views as a teacher. Question 2 may be a repetition of question 2 in **Silence is golden**, but it is a point worth insisting on. Question 6 can be done as a group activity, and should give you a chance to find out what you can and cannot discuss with this group. Then do the listening exercise.

Listening

- Students hear the same speakers as in the first listening exercise talking about what people do and do not talk about in their countries. Use this as a stimulus to get students discussing what they do and do not like talking about. Show students the subject index to this book and ask them to decide which topics they would enjoy discussing and which ones they certainly wouldn't want to discuss. Note their comments down for use when deciding what topics to cover in the future.

1 We talk about family, we talk about our job, we talk about friendship, money, success, sometimes religion, but not from the philosophical point of view, but as a social belief, as a habit; we won't talk about sex, we won't talk about child abuse for example, we won't talk about social problems.

2 Mostly they talk about the daily events or what has happened or, like, – if there is a wedding, somebody who has fallen sick, or somebody who has died. And local people hardly ever talk about politics because it doesn't much touch them. We don't usually talk of sex openly, and even parents don't explain to their children about sex.

Extra

- Brainstorm students on what kind of things annoy them when they're talking to someone. Write the items on the board. Now add any items from the list below that students have not mentioned, and get them to decide their own annoyance classification.

In a survey done in America these are the things that people find the most annoying, in order of annoyance. Students should note the very low annoyance level of items 8 and 10, and the relatively high positions of 3 and 5 which are common problems with non-native language speakers.

1 *Interrupting while others are talking*   **2** *Swearing*
3 *Mumbling or talking too softly*   **4** *Talking too loudly*
5 *Monotonous, boring voice*   **6** *Using filler words ('you know', 'like')*   **7** *Talking too fast*   **8** *Poor grammar, mispronunciation*
9 *A high-pitched voice*   **10** *A foreign or regional accent*

3 Toeing the line

1 What kind of mentality do the people have? How would you feel living in such a society?

2 Why is it useful to work out your own ideas rather than following the generally or officially accepted views?

3 How important is it to show people respect in a discussion? To what extent should this respect be taken?

4 Why do people discuss things?

5 How can you involve reticent speakers in your discussion?

> Discussion as an end in itself or as a method of practising the language is rarely seen as either enjoyable or useful. Students are encouraged to believe that there are correct answers and solutions to all problems. The culture here also tends not to reward independence of thought, individualism or any departure from the socially accepted norms. Furthermore, it is debatable to what extent conversation is valued as part of their culture, especially conversation of a discursive nature. Generally most people here tend to take their lead from the person who has the most status in any given situation rather than work out their own thoughts on something and try to persuade others to agree.

4 Devil's advocate

1 What is the difference between a conversation and a discussion? And between speak and talk?

2 Is discussion as an end in itself useful? Why? Why not?

3 What is the point in playing the devil's advocate? Have you ever played at being the devil's advocate either in a discussion or with a friend?

4 What is brainstorming? Why is it used and does it produce good results?

> In Ancient Greece, Socrates' way of initiating a discussion was to begin with some statement and then get the participants to think of every possible consequence of that statement in a logical sequence until they could prove that the statement was not true. Aristotle refined this system. Again he provided a statement, for example 'water is wet', but this time the participants had to think of arguments for and against that statement; then finally they reached some kind of conclusion. A variation of these systems is what is known as playing the devil's advocate. The Devil's Advocate was originally a Roman Catholic official, whose role was to examine the life and miracles of someone who had been nominated for becoming a saint. The official had to find out everything that was unfavourable to the case so that it could be taken into account before a final decision was made. These kinds of tactics are now sometimes known as 'reverse brainstorming', the idea being to think of as many reasons for an idea or plan failing rather than succeeding.

5 Taking turns

1 Which are the three most important criteria for having a discussion? Can you add any of your own?

2 Why is it important to have discussions during class time?

3 Is it better to have whole class discussions or group discussions?

4 During a discussion should the teacher express his/her opinion, i.e. be actively involved in the discussion?

5 If mistakes are made what should the teacher do?

6 What things would you never talk about:
  a   with a stranger?
  b   with a member of your family?
  c   with your best friend?
  d   with your partner?
  e   with members of this class?

> The class was asked to suggest the criteria for a good discussion. The children decided to write them in the order they thought would happen during a discussion. Their final list was as follows:
>
> to explain well
>
> listen to other people
>
> take turns to talk
>
> wait until the other person finishes
>
> say things which help other people
>
> keep to the subject
>
> share ideas with the rest of the group
>
> give suggestions and ideas
>
> be careful how you say things so that other people won't get upset
>
> ask each other questions so as to make things clear
>
> try not to be bossy in the group

Utopia

Warm-up

- Brainstorm students on things they'd like to see changed in their school, town, country, or the world in general, but that they have little hope of ever happening. Elicit the word 'utopia' as an ideal place where everyone is happy and things work efficiently. Ask if anyone knows the origin and meaning of 'utopia' (see ⓘ below). Now tell students that they are going to form their own Utopia. Write the following topics on the board: religion, law and crime, political parties, immigration, freedom of speech, working hours, dirty jobs, money, foreign policy.

- In groups of four, students now discuss the goals of their Utopia using the above topics as reference points, and adding any other considerations they feel relevant.

1   More's utopia

- Explain briefly who More was if you haven't already done so. Students should then match the extracts with the topics outlined in the warm-up (where possible) and then discuss More's ideas. NB Several questions may be answered in one extract.

🔑 **1** *law and crime*   **2** *religion*   **3** *political parties*   **4** *dirty jobs*
5 *working hours, money*   **6** *foreign policy.*

ⓘ The word 'utopia' first appeared in 1516 when an English lawyer/philosopher, Sir Thomas More, published a short book in Latin 'concerning the best state of a commonwealth and the new island Utopia'. Utopia is actually a fusion of the Greek words 'ou' (not) and 'topos' (place), and is probably a pun on another Greek word 'eutopia' meaning a 'happy place'. His ideas were a continuation of Plato and Aristotle's discussions on an ideal land. More expounded some intriguing ideas on marriage: Women can marry at 18, men at 22. Punishment for sex before marriage is being forbidden to marry for the rest of your life. The reason they punish this offence so severely is that they suppose few people would join in married love – with confinement to a single partner and the petty annoyances that married life involves – unless they were strictly restrained from promiscuity. Before getting married, each partner is shown nude to the other, so that each can be sure that there is no deformity lurking under their prospective spouse's clothing. Divorce is deliberately made difficult.

Listening

- Students listen to more of More's utopian ideas. Before they listen, dictate the questions **1–8** (above right). As a whole class, ask students to predict the answers to **1–5**.

Questions: True or False? **1** No travelling without government's permission. **2** Cities all look the same. **3** Everyone wears the same clothes, the only difference being between men and women. **4** Everyone usually eats together in a big canteen. **5** There are no bars or pubs. **6** What were the houses and gardens like? **7** What do people do in their free time? **8** Who is Hythloday and what does he think about Utopia?

🔑 **1–5** *all true*   **6** *all the same, no locks, doors open easily and close automatically, competition in gardens*   **7** *lectures, conversation, music*   **8** *guide who thinks Utopia is absurd*

Follow-up

- After listening, students draw some conclusions about whether More's Utopia really was a Utopia in our sense of the word (literary critics of Utopia are still baffled by some of More's ideas, and not least by Hythloday's comments at the end of the book).

🎧 A .. they actually take their clothes off?

B Yep!

A Wow, that's really weird.

B Well, actually the whole thing's pretty bizarre. You know they can't even travel without permission from the government, and even then if they stay in another place for more than a couple of days they have to work there.

A Sounds more like *1984* than Utopia.

B Exactly, and then everything looks the same.

A What do you mean?

B Well the cities are all built to the same plan, at least as far as possible they are.

A Well at least you'd never get lost if you did visit another town.

B Then everyone wears the same clothes, the only differentiation is between men and women.

A Well, like a kind of uniform?

B I guess so. And then everyone eats together in big halls where the food is prepared by the women.

A Some utopia.

B Well, Sir Thomas More was a man after all. But you could eat at home if you liked.

A So what about the houses, are they all the same too?

B Pretty much. Actually they had no locks on the doors; in fact the front doors are made so that they swing open easily and shut automatically. The only thing that seems different, or for that matter remotely competitive, is the gardens.

A The gardens?

B Yes, the citizens compete to see who can cultivate the best garden.

(The tapescript is continued on page 90.)

Utopia

✳ ✳ ✳

1   Serious offending is punishable with slavery, as this is more of a deterrent than death, and is also beneficial to the community. Attempted crimes are punished in the same way as committed ones. No lawyers because it's quicker and just as efficient if the accused plead their own case. The laws are very few anyway.⟮

2   The most important part of human happiness consists of pleasure, to lead a life as free of anxiety and as full of joy as possible, and to help everyone else towards that end. Virtue is rewarded and vice punished in the afterlife. Women can become priests. There are different sects and so no images of the gods are seen in the churches, people are thus not conditioned into seeing God in one particular way. Fortune-telling and any other superstitious divinations are held in ridicule and contempt.⟮

3   A prince is elected by the senate. No decisions about public matters can be made until they've been discussed in senate on three different days. Such matters can only be discussed in the senate; anyone who talks about them outside is put to death. This is supposed to stop people from conspiring against the government. There are no chances for corruption; no hiding places; no spots for secret meetings.⟮

4   Slaves are used to do any unpleasant or heavy chores, and kill animals. Killing animals is considered to be the first step on the road to killing men and hunting is immoral. Slaves mainly come from prisoners caught in wars, or are ex-criminals. You cannot be born a slave and you are free to leave Utopia whenever you want.⟮

5   There is no private business. Only six hours a day for working (or less if there's no work to be done), because everyone works hard and there's no need for intermediary professions like money-lenders and lawyers. People alternate between living in the country and living in the town, so that no-one will have to do heavy labour in the fields for more than two years (unless they want to). There is no money, anything you need you are provided with. Silver and gold are only used to buy things from foreign countries and to pay any mercenaries who may be needed to fight wars. In fact, any criminals are adorned in silver and gold as a sign of disgrace.⟮

6   It's acceptable to invade another country if they are not exploiting their land to its best advantage, to protect oppressed people, and obviously for defence. Very fierce mercenaries are used to conduct such wars. One seventh of extra produce is given freely to the poor of neighbouring countries and everything else at low prices.⟮

Continuation of tapescript from **1 More's Utopia**

A So what else did they do with their free time? I mean you said they only work six or seven hours a day, right?

B Yeah. They spend most of their time in intellectual activities, public lectures and so on; otherwise they just converse or listen to music.

A Well, what about bars, pubs, gambling, that kind of thing?

B No that's strictly out.

A Doesn't sound much fun at all.

B Well, from what I gathered from the introduction to the book, many critics don't really seem to know what's going on in the book at all. I mean the reader is accompanied round the island by this traveller, who has some unpronounceable name, Hythloday or something or other, which in Greek means an 'expert in nonsense' and one of his final comments is 'I was left thinking that quite a few of the laws and customs were really absurd'.

A No kidding!

2   Ideals

- Introduce this exercise by talking about ideals (thus linking the conversation back to the utopia idea). For example, is it important to have ideals? What makes people strive for their ideals? What are the characteristics of an idealist?

- Now on a more light-hearted note students do the quiz (choosing one answer only apart from in question 6) and discuss their answers in pairs.

3   The ideal student?

- Tell students to look at the descriptions of students on their page. Tell them that these were written by various English language teachers and that their task is to identify which sentences refer to ideal students (+) and which to totally non-ideal students (–). They should also think about which teachers they would and would not like to be taught by.

Listening

- Students hear follow-up sentences to the ones that appear on their page. They have to match the follow-up with the original. They then have to reassess their original answers and confirm which teachers they'd (not) like to be taught by and why.

1 *f* –   2 *d* +   3 *g* +   4 *j* –   5 *a* –   6 *c* –   7 *b* –   8 *h* ?

 1 I mean the fact is that we do. There's little logic in the use of prepositions.

2 I really believe that you can't learn a language without understanding something about the people who speak that language.

3 They really keep me on the ball. I sometimes have to tell them 'I'll write that down' and then go into the staff room at the end of the lesson and look up the problem in some grammar and tell them the next day. I find that really stimulating.

4 I find them so annoying. To be honest outside the lessons I prefer to talk to my students in Spanish. We are in Spain after all. Otherwise I feel like I'm at work.

5 Why people have to translate their names I don't know. It's OK with young kids, but with adults I ask you.

6 These kinds of students obviously have something to prove. Actually they're generally the ones that no-one else likes but are always the last to go at Christmas parties, if you know what I mean.

7 I try to tell them that they should concentrate on getting the gist of what was said.

8 To be honest I'm getting sick of teaching, with all this one-to-one stuff, but having a pretty face in front of you makes all the difference.

Writing

- Students describe their ideal teacher. They could use their compositions in the next lesson as the basis for a discussion on what makes a good student and what makes a good teacher. Other elements that you might like to discuss (depending on how confident you are of your own abilities!), how well teachers give instructions and explanations (and what students do if they don't understand these), what annoying mannerisms certain teachers have, and whether teachers in monolingual classes should ever speak in the students' mother tongue.

Utopia

2   Ideals

 Where is your ideal holiday?
- by the sea
- in the mountains
- visiting towns and museums

 Is your ideal friend...?
- sincere and honest
- intelligent
- charming and beautiful

 Is your ideal job...?
- very well paid but boring
- not very well paid but very interesting

 Is your ideal house...?
- a cottage in the country
- a farm
- a villa by the sea
- a penthouse in the town

 Is your ideal weekend spent with...?
- friends
- family
- just you and your partner

 Does your ideal disco have...? (choose 2)
- several dancing floors with different music
- one dancing floor with one type of music
- free entrance but expensive drinks
- expensive entrance and free drinks

 Are your ideal parents...?
- strict but fair
- easy going but without giving guidance

 Is your ideal school...?
- this one
- another one

3   The ideal student?

a The ones who introduce themselves saying: 'Hello my name's John' and you say 'Was one of your parents English?' thinking that their name really is 'John' and not 'Jean' or 'Jan' or whatever.

b Those that always want to know what every single word means.

c The kind that answers questions which were obviously intended for another student.

d Someone who takes a real interest not just in the language but in the culture as well.

e Ones that do their homework not because they have to but because they want to.

f Students who ask ridiculous questions, like why we say to think 'about' rather than to think 'to'.

g Students who ask difficult questions that really test your knowledge.

h As long as they're reasonably young and very attractive, I really couldn't care how good or bad their English is.

i Ones that are incredibly attentive about getting every word they say as grammatically correct as possible.

j People who insist on talking to you in English even when they meet you in the street.

Value

(i) This unit is based on three broad definitions of value –
moral values (i.e. what people consider to be right or wrong),
utility/importance (i.e. if something is worth doing/having),
and economic/material value (i.e. the monetary worth
people attach to certain objects; combined with this is the
affective value people attach to objects which may in fact be
totally worthless).

Warm-up

- What do students understand by the word 'value'? Get them
to write a few dictionary-type definitions. Choose a few
students and write their definitions on the board. Encourage
other students to improve or alter (if necessary) the
definitions to make them both more accurate and more
dictionary like. Make sure students' definitions cover the
three areas from the (i) above. Alternatively, brainstorm
students on the word 'value' and then categorise as
suggested in the (i) .
- Bring in some personal items (watch, jewellery, photos of
your house etc.) and get students to guess how much they
are economically and sentimentally worth. Alternatively
students do this amongst themselves with objects or photos
that they have brought in.
- Students now write down the four most valuable things they
have, either in terms of objects, skills or people, and discuss
whether these things are invaluable or not (i.e. whether it
would be possible to live without them). Ask students to add
a few more items to their list and see if they can assign a
monetary value to them or if they can find some viable
swaps with their partner's items.

1   Which do you value more?

- Students answer questions individually, then discuss the
answers in groups.

2   How strong are your moral values?

- Get students to discuss the following points regarding
moral values: **1** Is it important to have certain values and
principles? What are students' values? **2** Have people's
values changed over the generations? (e.g. What things do
our parents and did our grandparents value?) If so, how?
3 Do students' values conflict with those of people around
them? **4** Do they put their principles into action?
- Now tell students to look at the ten situations. Students are
to evaluate them in terms of how right or wrong they think
they are. They should use a mark ranging from **1** (perfectly
acceptable) to **5** (totally unacceptable). Students should do
this individually, then follow it with a group discussion.
- Alternatively, give students the title of the quiz and then get
them to invent their own questions, which they then try out
on each other.

Follow-up

- Get students to discuss Butler's quotation and to decide
whether morality changes from country to country,
generation to generation, and to compare their view of
morality with their parents' and grandparents' generations.

(i) Butler (English writer, painter 1835–1902) also had this to
say: 'Morality turns on whether the pleasure precedes or
follows the pain. Thus, it is immoral to get drunk because
the headache comes after the drinking, but if the headache
came first, and the drunkenness afterwards, it would be
moral to get drunk'.

Value

1 Which do you value more?

Which do you value more?

1 Your sense of taste or smell?

2 Your mind or your body?

3 Your arms or your legs?

4 Your own happiness or your (future) child's happiness?

5 Your friends or your family?

6 Your job or your dreams?

7 What you've received or what you've given?

8 Your money or your spirit?

9 Your religion or your citizenship?

10 This life or the next?

2 How strong are your moral values?

> Morality is the custom of one's country and the current feeling of one's peers. Cannibalism is moral in a cannibal country.
>
> (*Samuel Butler*)

1 Kidnapping and holding a child for ransom.

2 Politicians, to get money for themselves, using their influence to get a law passed which they know to be against the public's interest.

3 Smoking in lifts.

4 Buying stolen goods.

5 Newspapers treating crime as news so as to make a known criminal appear heroic.

6 Driving while well over the legal limit of alcohol.

7 Not voting in a national election.

8 Tax evasion by withholding important information.

9 Cheating on your partner.

10 Keeping £10 of extra change given by a clerk by mistake.

Value

3 You're the judge

- Tell students that an American psychologist, Kohlberg, made up some moral judgement stories, to evaluate adult morality. Students read one of these stories and then answer the questions that follow.
- Students must understand meaning of the text before answering the questions. They should think about the answers alone and then discuss them in pairs.

(i) (c) This idea can be extended to AIDS. Do pharmaceutical companies have a right to make a profit out of the millions afflicted with AIDS who are desperate to prolong their lives?
(j) What are the implications of letting Heinz go free?
Get class feedback on this.

Listening

- Students hear one person's answers to some of the questions on their page. Their task is to match the answers with the questions.

1 *i* **2** *a, b* **3** *f* **4** *c* **5** *j*

1 It's impossible to say really, I mean I think you have to be in that situation to say what you would actually do, but I think I'd do pretty much anything to save my own life as long as I didn't put anyone else's life in danger by doing so.

2 You can't really blame him can you? And as for the next question 'would a good husband do it?', well I know I would.

3 No, I think in this case, if it were for someone I didn't know very well, then I wouldn't take the risk. I mean they could get someone else to do it for them.

4 This really depends on your conscience doesn't it? I think that pharmaceutical companies make vast profits by first making us want to buy and then actually selling us a whole host of medicines that we'd probably be better off without. But in this case, I suppose there was nothing to stop him, just his conscience as I said before.

5 This all depends on how much you take the circumstances into account. But anyway if they let him off then that sets a precedent doesn't it? And then you could justify some addict throwing a brick through some chemist's window, just to get himself a …

4 Research

- In groups students imagine that they are members of a government agency which only has enough money to fund two of the projects. Firstly, students discuss the value of such projects, secondly which two not to fund, and finally compare their decisions with other groups.

(i) The Grand Canyon idea sounds absurd, but more than absurd it would be catastrophic. If followed through, the gold market would crash with inevitable consequences on other money markets, the prestige value of gold would disappear as it would no longer be a precious metal, jewellers would have to find other metals to use, etc.

An analysis of square fruit could be made from three main viewpoints. 1) Economic and Social: The most obvious benefit is in packaging – you can store far more in the same space, though to prevent rotting some kinds of fruit should not be in direct contact with each other. The immediate consequence would be a fall in transportation costs (and perhaps in the final cost of the fruit) which would make it difficult for traditional round fruits to compete, thus leading to massive square-fruit farming, ultimately eliminating small producers. Fruit sellers would benefit in terms of displaying the fruit, and juice makers and restaurants could exploit the square form to produce new and easier peeling methods.
2) Feasibility: It's difficult for square fruit to hang easily on branches, which leads to the question 'Why is fruit round?' Fruit is round so that when it falls it rolls: first, so as to limit the damage on impact to its skin (square fruit with all its corners would be considerably more susceptible to damage) and secondly so that the seeds roll away sufficiently far from their original tree as to not be obstructive when they in turn produce a new tree. Square fruit also has a greater surface area and is therefore more exposed to environmental hazards. The public, however, might find a square pear rather difficult to hold and to put in their mouths. 3) Ethics: Genetically engineered fruit is just the first step in rearranging nature to conform to our needs. Next we have square chickens (tiny head and no wings – already tried but with limited success as the idea is offputting) and then square people (again much easier to transport and design for – standard chairs, beds etc.)!

3 You're the judge

In Europe, a woman was near death from a particular kind of cancer. There was one drug that the doctors thought might save her. It was a form of radium that a druggist in the same town had recently discovered. The drug was expensive to make, but the druggist was charging ten times what the drug cost him to make. He paid $200 for the radium and charged $2,000 for a small dose of the drug. The sick woman's husband, Heinz, went to everyone he knew to borrow money, but he could only get together about $1,000, which is half of what it cost. He told the druggist that his wife was dying, and asked him to sell it cheaper or let him pay later. But the druggist said, 'No, I discovered the drug and I'm going to make money from it.' So Heinz got desperate and broke into the man's store to steal the drug for his wife.

a Should Heinz have done that? Was it actually wrong or right? Why?

b Is it a husband's duty to steal the drug for his wife, if he can get it no other way? Would a good husband do it?

c Did the druggist have the right to charge so much when there was no law setting a limit on the price? Why?

d If the husband does not feel very close or affectionate to his wife, should he still steal the drug?

e Suppose it wasn't Heinz's wife who was dying of cancer, but it was Heinz's best friend. His friend didn't have any money, and there was no-one in his family willing to steal the drug. Should Heinz steal the drug for his friend? Why?

f Suppose it was a person whom he knew that was dying but who was not a good friend. There was no-one else who could get him the drug. Would it be right to steal it for him? Why?

g What is there to be said on the side of the law in this case?

h Would you steal the drug to save your wife's life? Why?

i If you were dying of cancer but were strong enough, would you steal the drug to save your own life?

j Heinz broke into the store and stole the drug and gave it to his wife. He was caught and brought before the judge. Should the judge send Heinz to jail for stealing, or should he let him go free? Why?

4 Research

Without scientific progress the national health would deteriorate; without scientific progress we could no longer hope for improvement in our standard of living or for an increased number of jobs for our citizens; and without scientific progress we could not have maintained our liberties against tyranny.

(*V. Bush, U.S. presidential science adviser*)

1 A group of marine archaeologists have found Atlantis.

2 A group of genetic engineers have developed a way to produce square fruit.

3 A group of metallurgists and alchemists claim that they can convert the Grand Canyon into gold.

4 These computer scientists have developed a system for people to learn anything without having to study.

War

1 The art of war

- Brainstorm students on the causes of war. Now get them to read the statements on their page and decide which are causes and which are justifications – this will obviously depend on students' own interpretations.
- Alternatively, before beginning exercise, write up the following quotation on the board: 'War. What is it good for? Absolutely nothing.' (from a Bruce Springsteen song). Get students to analyse the wars of recent times. Did no good at all come from them? What might have happened if there hadn't been a war?

Writing

- Students discuss one of these two issues. (a) A just war is better than an unjust peace. (b) It's better to die with honour than to live with shame.

2 War crimes

- Some students may find this exercise sensitive.

- Give students these instructions: You are members of a cour martial. Your job is to try these 'war criminals' and decide if they are innocent or guilty; all are from your own country apart from cases **9** and **10**. What sentence would you give them? Students do this activity in groups.

- (2) If students say that torture is justified in this case (and remember it goes against the Geneva Convention), ask them to imagine the same situation but in this case the torturers didn't get the information they needed (although they were still sure the enemy soldier had the information they wanted). (5) A World War II general cites cannibalism as behaviour that has 'a bad effect on troop morale'. (8) The results of horrendous tests carried out in concentration camps, were then used for many years after the war to help underwater divers resist the cold and water pressure. Does the end justify the means?

Follow-up

- Does the *method* of killing someone in war affect students' views? (e.g. chemical weapons, nuclear bomb, hand-to-hand combat etc.).

1 The art of war

> Men appear to prefer ruining one another's fortunes, and cutting each other's throats about a few paltry villages, to extending the grand means of human happiness.

(*Voltaire*)

1 Adam and Eve fell from God's grace. One of the results of their fall was that Cain murdered his brother Abel, and people haven't stopped killing each other since.

2 A political means to stop the masses from thinking about other things (e.g. economic problems at home).

3 Basically we all fear each other: if I don't kill you first, you will kill me.

4 A means of preventing invasion and stopping other wars.

5 A way to provide a lot of people with jobs (soldiers, workers in the arms industry).

6 The world population can be kept down.

7 An occupation for some men who are unable to do anything else but play at soldiers.

8 A means of upholding certain moral, political or religious principles.

9 A noble means of spending one's time full of excitement, expectation and glory.

10 It gives people a sense of purpose and makes them brave and patriotic.

11 In several parts of the world, evidence has been found that our predecessors, a kind of killer ape, actually ate each other. The skill they learned in killing each other – an accurate hit on the head with the shoulder blade of an antelope for example – required considerable co-ordination. It was as a result of this that man's brain developed. This hunting instinct then turned onto other men, horses were used for mobility and the art of war had begun.

2 War crimes

1 This soldier deserted during a battle to defend your country.

2 As a last resort, these men brutally tortured an enemy soldier to get information which eventually saved the lives of 20,000 civilians (including members of your family).

3 These soldiers raped women from enemy villages.

4 This doctor used the organs of captured dying enemy soldiers to save the lives of your soldiers.

5 These soldiers, cut adrift by their leaders, consumed the flesh of comrades and enemy soldiers killed in fighting.

6 These peace demonstrators broke into a prisoner-of-war camp and set free 1,000 enemy soldiers.

7 These soldiers forced prisoners of war to endure a tortuous 260 km march on which anyone who dropped out of line was immediately shot.

8 These scientists conducted cruel experiments on prisoners of war, the results of these experiments are now saving many lives.

9 This enemy pilot dropped a bomb on one of your cities causing the death of 100,000 inhabitants.

10 This enemy general ordered the kidnapping of hundreds of children from your country, so that they could be 're-educated' in his country.

War

3 Mines

- In groups, students read text and decide which statements they agree with and why.

(i) Land mines make vast areas of agricultural land unworkable. In Cambodia 1 in 236 citizens are amputees, making them unable to work and support their families, as well as being a heavy burden on the state. In Kuwait the number of deaths involved in clearing the mines cost one third of the total lives lost in the war itself. 96 manufacturers in 48 countries manufacture five to ten million antipersonnel land mines each year, generating up to $200 million in sales. One manufacturer is promoting a device that is mounted on vehicles and sprays as many as 30 land mines per second. In ten years producers hope to offer a 'smart' land mine that can co-ordinate detonation with adjacent mines to achieve optimum killing efficiency. One proposal for reducing the destruction caused by mines is to require manufacturers to install a self-deactivation mechanism in all land mines.

(4) From 1944–1950, the French forced German prisoners of war to play the leading role in minesweeping operations on the Normandy beaches and other battlefields, 1,709 were killed and nearly 3,000 wounded (471 French personnel were also killed).

Writing

- Students discuss the following question: Imagine you live in a country infested with mines, what would be the consequences on your life and of those around you?

4 The cost of war

- Students underline what they think is the correct figure. Obviously they cannot be expected to know the answers, but by guessing them they are more motivated into listening for the correct answer.

Listening

- Students hear the true figures and compare with their guesses.

🔊 **1** 20 **2** minute **3** 30 **4** 15 **5** 56% **6** 20% **7** 300
8 200; only Costa Rica and Iceland have no military forces.

📼 A That's incredible, look, more than 20 million people have been killed in war since 1945.
B But that doesn't include the Second World War does it?
A No. God this is appalling, we've got enough bombs and arms to kill everyone on the planet 300 times over.

B And look at this, twenty per cent of scientists and engineers involved in arms development, it makes you think doesn't it, if we invested all that time and money in peaceful enterprises.
A What about this? Guess which are the only two countries that have no military forces.
B No idea. What are they?
A Costa Rica and Iceland.
B I thought Switzerland was supposed to have no army.
A This is terrible. Read this.
B In the Iran-Iraq war fifteen countries supplied weapons to both sides.' But who are all these countries?
A Ah! Look! See I told you there were about thirty wars being fought every day. But I certainly got this one wrong, we spend nearly two million dollars a minute on war.
B I wonder how they calculate that.
A Well however they do it, it's a very telling figure. Just think what could be done with all that money.
B And Ethiopia spent just over half of its entire national budget on military defence in 1989.
A What was going on in 1989? It seems so long ago I can't even remember.
B I wanted to know about the tonnes of fissionable products, ah! here it is. Good grief! Two hundred million tonnes.
A It really makes you think doesn't it?

Follow-up

- Get students to think about the implications of these statistics. How could the money wasted in war be better spent? Is it morally acceptable to supply both sides in a war with weapons? Is scientific research into arms necessarily always a bad thing?

Extra

- Students imagine they're preparing a nuclear bunker, i.e. a fortified place underground where people can protect themselves in the event of a nuclear attack. What would they take with them and what people with particular professions might be needed? Would they be able to justify their own presence?

- In groups, students discuss the relative merits of military service. In a multilingual class students can discuss how military/civil service functions in their country. Is there anything they would die for? Is there anything they would kill for? If their country had been destroyed would they press the button to obliterate the attacking enemy nation?

Writing

- Students discuss the following question: What are the qualities of a conscientious objector, a general, and a mercenary?

3 Mines

A TYPICAL ANTIPERSONNEL LAND MINE IS an innocuous-looking piece of plastic that weighs about a kilogram, fits in the palm of the hand and costs only a couple of dollars to manufacture. When stepped on, it explodes with enough force to rip the legs off an adult or reduce a small child to pulp. Those not killed by the blast or loss of blood frequently succumb to infections caused by shrapnel forced deep into body tissues. Rarely in the annals of human conflict has there been a simpler way of killing or maiming so many.

Though many regional conflicts are over, the mines remain – millions of them. According to US and UN estimates, between 85 million and 100 million antipersonnel land mines lie scattered in 62 countries; as many are presently stockpiled. The estimated bill for the worldwide clean-up is $85 billion or more, and that does not include the huge cost of assisting victims in need of hospital treatment and rehabilitation.

1 Mines should be banned in the same way as biological and chemical weapons, but no government would agree to this.

2 Mines are a cheap way for poor countries to defend themselves.

3 Civilians who have lost limbs due to mines exploding should receive compensation from the government who had the mines laid.

4 Prisoners of war from the nation that planted the mines should be employed to remove them.

5 Private companies who produce mines are in no way responsible for how these mines are used and the destruction they cause.

4 The cost of war

1 (10/20/200) million people have died in war since 1945.

2 The world spends more than $1.85 million a (minute/hour/day) on war.

3 In the past 15 years an average of (10/20/30) wars are being fought every day.

4 More than 40 countries supplied armaments in the Iran-Iraq war, (5/15/35) supplied to both sides.

5 In 1989 the Ethiopian government spent (26/56/76) per cent of its entire national budget on military defence.

6 About (10/20/50) per cent of the world's 2.5 million research scientists and engineers are engaged in arms development and improvement.

7 Millions of animals and plants are destroyed by bombing and chemical weapons, of which there are enough to kill everyone in the world (100/200/300) times over.

8 More than (50/100/200) million tonnes of radioactive fission products have been released into the atmosphere through testing nuclear bombs.

X-certificate

X-certificate generally refers to films that are considered by a board of censors to be unsuitable for minors. This unit extends this meaning to a variety of subjects where some form of censorship comes into play.

Warm-up

- Brainstorm students on impediments to freedom of expression in their country. Some areas that they should consider: 1) What documents are compulsory for citizens of students' countries? e.g. documents that are legally required at all times / for employment / when applying for a passport. 2) Are there any countries they are not allowed to visit? 3) What happens if they are found in possession of banned political literature / they refuse to do compulsory military service?
- Go to the section entitled **Declaration of human rights**.

1 Freedom of the press

- Students read the text and answer the questions in groups.

2 Cyberspace

- You may not wish to use this exercise with some students.

- Brainstorm students on what they consider to be indecent and offensive. List the students' suggestions on the board. Students use this list to create definitions for the words 'indecent' and 'offensive'. You might find that what some people consider to be offensive, others do not. If you are in a multilingual class be especially careful not to offend. For example women might be considered indecent if they show bare legs or arms in some countries, whereas in nudist camps it is acceptable to wear nothing at all. British people might find burping after a meal offensive whereas it is a sign of appreciation in other cultures.
- Students read the passage and discuss the questions.

(i) The punishment for indecency as outlined by the Communications Decency Act was a $250,000 fine plus a two-year prison sentence. Many school boards around the US had already removed famous nude paintings from classroom walls, banned the works of Twain, and tried to ban discussion on human reproduction. The law might have considerably reduced serious medical discussion on issues such as abortion, the side effects of Prozac, etc.

1 Freedom of the press

The first newspapers in Britain in the eighteenth and nineteenth century had an incredible number of taxes imposed on them. Most of these taxes were intended to limit circulation rather than raise money for the government, and were only abolished in 1861.

In the period of the Industrial Revolution there was a new thirst for knowledge, and cover prices were almost the equivalent of a labourer's daily wages. This meant that poor people didn't have enough money to buy newspapers and were thus deprived of vital information — a brilliant tactic by the wealthy classes to restrict trade unionism.

Nowadays, even in countries which believe they are the home of democracy, such as England, stringent constraints are imposed on the media. In 1992, an independent TV channel (Channel 4), reporting on controversial events in Northern Ireland, lost a court case in which they were forced to reveal the name of a source who had been critical of the Royal Ulster Constabulary (the police force in Northern Ireland).

Should the government be allowed to …

1 stop newspapers from releasing documents from the secret service relating to national security?

2 prevent the media from publishing embarrassing reports on the private lives of members of parliament?

3 stop newspapers from printing cartoons which ridicule members of parliament?

4 force the media to name their sources?

5 stop newspapers from publishing articles which are totally opposed to the government and which might incite civil disorder?

2 Cyberspace

IN 1996 A U.S. COURT PANEL made an important and controversial decision to block the Communications Decency Act. This Act had been recently introduced to prohibit the distribution of indecent material over the Internet and other computer networks which children might have access to. However the Act had not clearly defined what constituted 'indecent' and 'patently offensive' words or images.

Many people had objected to the Act on the grounds that some of the following might have been banned from the Internet: Michelangelo's *David*, Botticelli's *The Birth of Venus*; Mark Twain's *The Adventures of Huckleberry Finn*, Sophocles' *Oedipus Rex*; web pages discussing important issues such as The Breastfeeding Page, Information on Safer Sex, Family Planning and Fertility, The National Library of Medicine's view of the human body; lyrics to the songs of Alanis Morisette, Pearl Jam, Radiohead, etc.

The Federal Judges' court panel had this to say in defence of their decision to block the Act: 'As the most participatory form of mass speech yet developed, the Internet deserves the highest protection from governmental intrusion.'

The Act would have had important global implications as it would have been the first time that a government had attempted to censor worldwide media. ∎

1 Do you agree with the judges' decision?

2 Whose responsibility is it to censor what children have access to?

3 Should there be censorship on what adults have access to?

4 Should one government have the right to censor material that would otherwise be available worldwide?

5 Do you use the Internet? What for? How well does it work?

6 What things do you think the Internet will be used for in the future?

3 Dwarf throwing

- Tell students to read the text (which is all true), but not to answer the questions. Then brainstorm them on what it must have been like for the dwarfs and how they (i.e. the students) would have felt in the same situation. Follow this discussion with the listening exercise and then the questions that follow the text.

Listening

- Students listen to an Australian, Dave, describing his experience, and answer these questions:

Questions: 1 How did Dave get involved in dwarf throwing? **2** What protection did they use after the first time? **3** Why did the 'humanitarians' object to dwarf throwing and how did they find out about it? **4** Did they understand dwarf problems? **5** What kinds of things are humiliating for dwarfs? **6** What were the good points about dwarf throwing?

1 *by challenging two big guys* **2** *helmets, arm and knee pads* **3** *humiliating for the dwarfs; through a newspaper article* **4** *no* **5** *no consideration from other people, teasing, few job opportunities* **6** *money, recognition, respect, favourable newspaper articles*

I suppose it all began as a kind of joke. Me and a couple of mates were in this pub in Sydney and I suppose we'd all had a bit too much to drink. Anyway we were standing next to these two big guys and we could hear them talking about us. They were betting on how far they reckoned they could throw us. So I turned round and said to them: 'no way can you throw us that far'; because they'd been saying they could throw us right across the room. And they said: you wanna bet? And that's how it all began, though the first time we didn't do it inside the pub, but outside in the garden so that we'd have a reasonably soft landing. Next time we kitted ourselves out with helmets, and arm and knee pads, bit like American footballers, and these big guys would hurl us onto mattresses. Within a few weeks hundreds of people were coming to watch and by this time there were about twenty dwarfs involved. And of course we were all being paid. Good money too. And then they came along, the do-gooders,

the humanitarians, the ones who know what's best for others. They said it was humiliating for us to have ourselves thrown around a pub for the fun of others. But what did they know about humiliation? Were they dwarfs? No. Did they really understand our problems? No. Because if they really had been acting in our best interests then they would have left us alone. I can tell you that what is humiliating about being a dwarf is that no-one considers you, they just tease you, make stupid references to Snow White. And the chances of you ever getting a job are minimal. And here we were for the first time in our lives actually making some good money. We had a sense of recognition, of fulfilment. There was this feeling of mutual respect between us and the big guys who were throwing us. We were in the papers. We were being talked about. And the good thing was that journalists were not only writing about the throwing competitions in the pubs, but they'd also begun writing about our problems and our role in society. And it was ironically as a result of some busybody reading one of these articles, that someone from some government department was sent down to one of the pubs. She decided that the sport should be banned and within a few weeks we were all out of a job again.

- Students then discuss the questions beside the text.

4 Human rights

- Do question 1 as whole class activity, to test out how liberal your students are. If the general consensus is that none of these rights should be infringed on, tell students to move directly on to the next questions and to discuss them in groups.

(3) Students could imagine they are dictators and imagine all the ways they could impinge on their citizens' rights and privacy. (4) Law-enforcement agencies say they need tapping to keep tabs on drug runners, terrorists and spies.

In Great Britain the freedom to move in one's own country is sometimes infringed: the Home Secretary under the Prevention of Terrorism Act may confine suspects (which can affect families) to either Northern Ireland or Great Britain. In the 1970s Britain was taken to the European Court of Human Rights by the Irish government. The court condemned Britain for inhuman and degrading treatment.

X-certificate

3 Dwarf throwing

Until quite recently in some pubs in Australia you could see dwarfs being thrown from one end of the bar to the other by big muscled Aussies. 'Dwarf throwing competitions' attracted big crowds: the dwarfs were paid a lot of money to put on a crash helmet and allow themselves to be thrown onto a mattress, located some metres away. Few were hurt and most enjoyed their sudden rise to fame. A variation was 'dwarf bowling', popular in England too. This 'game' consisted of tying a dwarf to a skateboard and 'bowling' him (again equipped with a crash helmet) rather than a ball, down the alley and against the pins. For a while, dwarf throwing competitions were used under sponsorship to raise money for charity, but some people under the auspices of such groups as the Organisation of People of Restricted Growth objected to what they called these 'macabre spectacles'.

1 Were the 'human rights' activists right in having these activities banned, thus depriving the dwarfs of a lot of money and excitement?

2 What rights do we have in deciding what is right or best for other people?

3 Many people would agree that the following should be banned, try and think of reasons why they shouldn't be banned: casinos, hunting, the Klu Klux Klan and other racist/fascist groups, religious sects, satanic groups, smoking.

4 What would you like to ban in: your school, your town, your country, other countries?

4 Human rights

1 On the right, are some basic freedoms outlined in the Universal Declaration of Human Rights. Are there any situations where it would be justified to infringe these rights?

2 Can you think of any recent cases, in your country or others, where these rights have been infringed? Why did the government in question do this and were they justified?

3 What information does a government have a right to know about its people? For example, where you live, who you live with, if you're married, if you have a job, who your friends are, how often you leave the country, what your politics are, if you drink/smoke/take drugs, if you study English, etc.

4 Should governments be able to tap into every phone, fax and computer transmission? Why should they want to do this, and why should we as citizens not want this?

5 What information should be contained on someone's identity card (e.g. driving offences, criminal records, current account number)?

All human beings are born free and equal in dignity and rights. They are endowed with reason and conscience and should act towards one another in a spirit of brotherhood.

(Universal Declaration of Human Rights Article 1)

Freedom ...
1 To leave one's country
2 To seek information and teach ideas
3 Of peaceful political opposition
4 Of peaceful assembly and association
5 Of inter-racial, inter-religious and civil marriage
6 From compulsory religion or state ideology in schools
7 From police searches of home without warrant
8 From torture or coercion by state
9 Of all courts to total independence
10 From censorship of mail
11 To publish and educate in ethnic languages
12 From compulsory military service
13 To purchase and drink alcohol
14 To use contraceptive pills and devices
15 Of divorce (for men and women equally)

YOU

1 Hey you!

- Students look at the table and try and work out what language it is and what it means. Probably the only clue they may have is in the title of the unit! Explain that this table is from an Old English grammar (the thorn symbol was the OE's *th*). In Shakespeare's day, cases (nominative, accusative etc.) were still in use (*thou* indicated close familiarity or inferiority, 'you' was more impersonal and general), but not the dual form (i.e. used for addressing two people rather than one or more than two). Our current word *you* comes from the plural form in the table.
- Students should read the passage and answer the questions.

(i) In the seventeenth century *thou* and *you* became explicitly involved in social controversy. The Religious Society of Friends (or Quakers) was founded in the middle of this century by George Fox. One of the practices setting off this rebellious group from the larger society was the use of Plain Speech, and this entailed saying *thou* to everyone. George Fox explained the practice in these words:
'Moreover, when the Lord sent me forth into the world, He forbade me to put off my hat to any, high or low; and I was required to Thee and Thou all men and women, without any respect to rich or poor, great or small' (quoted in Estrich and Sperber, 1946).

Fox wrote a fascinating pamphlet (Fox , 1660), arguing that T (*tu*) to one and V (*vos*) to many is the natural and logical form of address in all languages. Among others he cites Latin, Hebrew, Greek, Arabic, Syriack, Aethiopic, Egyptian, French, and Italian. Fox suggests that the Pope, in his vanity, introduced the corrupt and illogical practice of saying V to one person. Farnsworth, another early Friend, wrote a somewhat similar pamphlet (Farnsworth, 1655), in which he argued that the Scriptures show that God and Adam and God and Moses were not too proud to say and receive the singular T.

For the new convert to the Society of Friends the universal T was an especially difficult commandment. Thomas Ellwood (1714) has described the trouble that developed between himself and his father:
'But whenever I had occasion to speak to my Father, though I had no Hat now to offend him; yet my language did as much: for I durst not say YOU to him, but THOU or THEE, as the Occasion required, and then would he be sure to fall on me with his Fists.'

As the passage on the student's page states, the *tu* (T form) and *vos* (V form), were originally singular and plural forms, respectively. The Roman emperor origin of the V form is only a conjecture but what is certain is that in a later period the aristocracy began using V forms to each other as a sign of respect, and T forms to the lower classes as a sign of power. The lower classes used T forms among themselves and V with superiors. Then the T form came to indicate solidarity. It was used by all people, irrespective of class, who felt some kind of similarity or intimacy. V forms were then used to symbolise all forms of social difference and distance.

Below is an extract from *Sociolinguistics* by Peter Trudgill which summarizes some work by Brown and Gilman on which the passage on the student's page is based:

Brown and Gilman have investigated the extent of T- and V-usage by students from different European and other countries. They found that relationships such as father–son, customer–waiter, boss–clerk were never 'power coded' in modern French, German or Italian. Pronoun usage was now always reciprocal, although formerly this would not have been the case. Afrikaans speakers, on the other hand, did make several non-reciprocal power-coded distinctions in these situations. This, according to Brown and Gilman, signifies a 'less developed egalitarian ethic' on the part of Afrikaans speakers. From their work and from other sources, it also appears that French and Italian speakers are more likely to use T to acquaintances than German speakers; that German speakers are more likely to use T to distant relations; Norwegian schoolchildren are more likely than Dutch or German pupils to use T to their teachers; male Italians are more likely than German and French males to use T to female fellow students; and generally, Italians use more T than the French, who in turn use more T than the Germans.

1 Hey you!

<table>
<tr><th colspan="4">SECOND PERSON</th></tr>
<tr><th></th><th>Singular</th><th>Dual</th><th>Plural</th></tr>
<tr><td>Nom.</td><td>þū,</td><td>git</td><td>gē</td></tr>
<tr><td>Acc.</td><td>þec, þē</td><td>inc, incit</td><td>ēowic, ēow, īow</td></tr>
<tr><td>Gen.</td><td>þīn</td><td>incer</td><td>ēower, īower</td></tr>
<tr><td>Dat.</td><td>þē</td><td>inc</td><td>ēow, īow</td></tr>
</table>

1 In your language how many equivalents of 'you' do you have?

2 What form would you use to your: mother, father, sister/brother, relative, teacher, friend, boss, priest, customer, waiter, lawyer, rubbish collector, doctor, someone from a different social class or caste?

3 Do we really need more than one form of 'you'? Why?

4 What other forms of address do you have (e.g. Sir, Madam, Professor, Doctor)? How often and on what occasions are these used?

5 In what other ways do you change your language (or register) in particular social contexts?

Addressing someone to their face in English couldn't be easier: we say *you* to everyone. But it wasn't always so simple as you can see from the table above. By Shakespeare's day, things were a little better – *thou* indicated close familiarity, anger or inferiority, whereas *you* was more impersonal and general.

Most European languages have at least two forms of *you*. In the Latin of antiquity there was only *tu* in the singular. The plural *vos* as a form of address to one person was originally only directed to the emperor. But when the empire was split in two, there were actually two emperors (ruling from Rome and Constantinople) so any words addressed to one man were, by implication, addressed to both. The choice of *vos* as a form of address may have been in response to this implicit plurality. An emperor is also plural in another sense; he is the summation of his people and can speak as their representative. Royal persons sometimes say *we* where an ordinary man would say *I*.

Sociologists tell us that the fact that we have only one form of you in English is a sign of how egalitarian our society is. Speakers in Asian countries, on the other hand, have a wide choice of forms to use depending on the social context. A Korean speaker, for example, may have to choose between six different verb suffixes (intimate, familiar, plain, polite, deferential, and authoritative).

However, this kind of language power game, i.e. you call me *vos*, and I'll call you *tu* because I am more important than you, still survives in English-speaking countries, where people often call their inferiors by their first name, whereas the latter use their superior's title and surname as a mark of respect. Blacks in America were used to this kind of behaviour, and still now in South Africa whites tend to call blacks by their first names, and not vice versa.

2 First names

- As an introduction to this exercise, and before giving students their photocopies give students these riddles: What is it that was given to you, belongs to you exclusively, and yet is used more by your friends than by you? (Your name) What is it that you must keep after giving it to someone else? (Your word) What can a man give to a woman that he can't give to a man? (His name) Now ask students to choose an English name for themselves. In groups they then discuss their names and why they chose them. Then do the listening, and finally students read text and discuss questions.

(i) Your name can influence other people's judgement of how attractive you are. In tests, male students have been given pictures of equally attractive girls, but with more or less attractive names (Kathy, Jennifer, Christine as opposed to Ethel, Harriet and Gertrude). Those with 'attractive' names were judged to be more physically attractive.

Listening

- Students hear a Ugandan and a Chinese woman explaining how names are given in their countries. Students' task is simply to listen for interest; some of what they hear is then repeated in the reading exercise.

1 In some parts of Africa children are considered, well a child born to a family, is considered a guest until he's five. And I think that comes mostly because of lots of infectious diseases children usually die early. If they die then they are considered that they didn't like the place where they were born, and I think it's also another way of accepting death. A child is considered a human being after he's five and that is when he is given a name.

2 All names can be composed taking, using normal words. And people tend, according to their cultural background, and educational background, normally we do tend to use things from nature, like trees for a boy, which means honesty, strength, and flowers for a girl, which means beauty, fragrance, delicacy.

3 Family names

- Students read the passage and answer the questions.

(i) Another origin of British surnames, and presumably other European names, is the parts people played in a pageant (e.g. Bishop, King, Pope).

4 *descriptive: Short, Moody, Brown; local: Lane, Wood; occupational: Carpenter, Butcher, Black(smith); patronymic: Peterson.*

Listening

- Students hear two people discussing what name a woman should adopt when she marries. They listen and answer these questions.

Questions: 1 Why did Su's mother invent her own surname, how did she choose it? **2** How did other feminists of Su's mother's generation choose their names? **3** What is Su's surname and why does she have this name? **4** What system do they use in Italy? **5** What is the disadvantage of, and solution to, this system?

1 *She wanted to liberate herself from male dominance, she chose the name of her own profession.* **2** *Choosing days of the week or the town where they were born.* **3** *Writer Wells, a combination of her parents' surnames.* **4** *Woman keeps maiden name, but children have father's name.* **5** *Children have father's name, son keeps father's name; daughter mother's.*

A I've often wondered, why you've got a double-barrelled surname, I mean you're American, and I thought it was only us Brits who went in for things like that. Susan Writer Wells, it sounds almost invented, doesn't it?

B Well, actually Jo you're not far off the mark. You know my mom was a feminist don't you? I mean like one of the original ones.

A Really? I never knew that. Well go on then.

B Yeah, well her maiden name was Morse or something, and at that time, I'm talking about the late sixties, women like my mom were really trying to liberate themselves from male bondage, as they called it. So some of them began rejecting their father's surname and decided to invent their own surname instead, and because mom was a journalist she decided to call herself Cindy Writer.

A Cindy Writer. Well, who would have guessed!

B Actually other feminists named themselves after the town where they were born, like the sculptor Judy Chicago. Some even called themselves after a day of the week.

A Oh, yes wasn't there someone called Nancy Friday? Or maybe she's got nothing to do with it. But your mum wasn't so much of a feminist that she didn't get married, was she?

B No. But the problem then was what to call herself or rather her children. Anyway a lot of people of her generation, and more especially of her way of thinking, simply decided to add their husband's name to their own. My dad's called Paul Wells, so I'm Su Writer Wells, though I can't say I'm too keen on it.

A So what would happen if you, Su Writer Wells, meet some guy who's called Peter Painter Jones, do you then become Su Writer Wells Painter Jones, bit of a mouthful isn't it?

B No comment. I think the most sensible thing to do is to do what they do in countries like Italy.

A What do you mean?

B Well there the woman keeps her maiden name pretty much for all purposes, like bank accounts, identity cards; and the man obviously keeps his name.

A What about the children?

B Well they keep their father's name.

A So we're back to the old problem, aren't we, the men win out again.

B Yeah, but one solution might be for the sons to keep their father's name and the daughter their mother's.

A Yes, good idea.

2 First names

1 Why did your parents give you your first name? Do you know the origin of your name? Does it have an equivalent in English? If not, how could you translate it?

2 Should we just be given temporary names until we are old enough to choose our own name?

3 Do you like your name? Would you change your name if you could? What famous people have changed their names? Why did they do it? Is the new name better than the original one?

4 What are your favourite names: (a) in your own language? (b) in English?

Throughout history names have often had a kind of magical quality. In some societies, Arab or Chinese, for example, a beautiful child may be called by a deprecating name – 'Dog', 'Stupid', 'Ugly', – in order to ward off the evil eye. Alternatively, two words may be combined together, e.g. gold and treasure, to produce a unique name, which it is hoped will bring its owner good luck.

In the West, names are very rarely unique — many parents still name their children after saints, though some might call a succession of children First, Second, Third (as in Italy). Some fathers simply name their children after themselves (Frank Sinatra junior), others take this to extremes — George Formby, the American heavyweight boxer, named five of his sons 'George'.

In Africa, however, many children are given unique names, and some have to wait several years before receiving one. Where child mortality is high, children are often treated as visitors to this planet, and are simply given a name which corresponds to how old they are. Then on their fifth birthday, they are considered as no longer being visitors, but have come to earth to stay, and it is only at this point that they are given a name. Not always a first name and a surname, but just one unique name. If, however, they die before they are five, then it is believed that they didn't like our planet and they have gone back to where they came from.

In modern society many artists, especially musicians and actors, actually change their names in the hope that it will bring them fortune — Madonna and Prince, for example; though Prince then began to refer to himself through a squiggly symbol rather than a name. Other rock stars have given their children strange names, Frank Zappa called two of his children Dweezil and Moon Unit; and David Bowie introduced the fashion for names like Ziggy.

More recently parents have tended to name their children after their idols — stars of the cinema and football — in the hope that some of the magic of these heroes and heroines will somehow be miraculously transferred to their offspring.

3 Family names

1 What origin does your surname have? How would you translate it into English? How many other names have you got? How many names do you need? What are the worst surnames in your country and why are they so bad?

2 Have you had any problems as a result of having the surname you were born with?

3 Have you got or had any nicknames? Did you like them? Were you ever teased?

4 Put the following English surnames into the right category: Lane, Peterson, Carpenter, Short, Butcher, Black, Moody, Brown, Wood.

5 When is using first names and surnames appropriate: (a) in England, America etc.? (b) in your own country?

6 Should women keep their maiden name when they get married? What other alternatives are there for married women?

In most countries people only used to have one name; for example, think of the important religious figures in your country's early history (Moses, Mahomet, Siddharta). Some people were identified by a single name of two elements, e.g. the Greek philosopher Aristo-cles (= of best renown) or the Slavonic Bogu-slav (= divine glory). Both the Romans and the Russians invented a threefold system for naming. In Rome a child was given one name nine days after birth, then an inherited family name and then some kind of epithet or nickname (e.g. Cicero = chick pea). The three names were then put together, e.g. Publius Ovidius Naso (nose), Nikita Sergeievich Khrushchev (first name, son of, surname).

British surnames fall into four main groups: descriptive (e.g. Arm-strong, Foot), local (Hall, Hill, [village] Green), occupational (Archer, Baker) and patronymic (Johnson = John's son, Macdonald = son of Donald, O'Connor = son of Connor). Being a 'son of' (or daughter of) a famous person (e.g. Lennon, Kennedy, Onassis) may open doors to you that might otherwise have remained shut; but it may mean that people expect too much of you too soon, or merely compare you unfavourably to your famous parent or relative, leaving you to spend the rest of your life proving yourself. In any case, this is certainly better than having no name at all, at least not officially. Until recently in South Africa not everyone had the right to a name and nationality; this caused considerable problems in the first elections which subsequently brought Mandela to power.

Zodiac

Warm-ups

- Ask a few students what signs they are. Ask everyone to write down their name and birthdate on a piece of paper and to give this paper to you. Pair some students up with the same sign and some with different signs (but don't tell students this). All pairs should now spend five or ten minutes finding out (and briefly listing) what they have in common. Then conduct a class survey to see if those of the same sign had more items on their list than those from different signs.

1 Star signs

- Students read the texts on their page and guess which one refers to their star sign.

🔑 **1** *Aries* **2** *Gemini* **3** *Taurus* **4** *Cancer* **5** *Virgo* **6** *Leo*
7 *Libra* **8** *Scorpio* **9** *Capricorn* **10** *Sagittarius*
11 *Aquarius* **12** *Pisces*

Listening

- Students listen to a phone-in interview with an astrologist and answer the questions.

Questions: **1** What is the origin of 'horoscope'?
2 Does Dr Starr believe in the validity of daily horoscopes?
3 How does Dr Starr account for the differences in twins?
4 How well does Dr Starr answer the third caller's question?
5 What is caller 4's question, how does Dr Starr answer it?

🔑 **1** *hour + watcher* **2** *no* **3** *ascending sign + free will*
4 *avoids question* **5** *influence of heredity, astrology predicts general framework within which there is free will.*

🔲 (A = interviewer; B = Dr Starr; C = callers)

A First of all let me thank you Dr Starr for joining us on tonight's 'The Sceptics Show'. Let's take the first listener's question — Mrs Quirk from Manchester asks:

C1 What is the origin of the word 'horoscope' and what does Dr Starr think of the horoscope predictions in daily newspapers?

A Yes, I've often wondered what horoscope meant.

B Well any students of Greek will know that it means 'observer of the hour of birth', from 'hora' meaning 'hour' and 'skopos' meaning 'watcher'. As for popular horoscopes — well, they are based almost exclusively on the position of the sun in the twelve signs of the zodiac, and I'd obviously agree that you can't make the same forecast for one twelfth of the world's population. However daily forecasts based on the sun, if sensibly interpreted ...

A Yes. We've got another caller on the line now, can we hear your question caller?

C2 Yes, I have a twin sister and I'd like to ask Dr Starr how she accounts for differences in twins who for all practical purposes are born at the same time.

B This is a difficult question but one which I can nevertheless answer. In astrology the ascending sign is very important and this changes its degree every four minutes, so there could be appreciable differences.

A Yes, what about Siamese twins? They're born at exactly the same time.

B Of course there is a spiritual factor in us, we all have our own free will, we are after all individuals.

A We have a caller on line three. What is your question please?

C3 I once read about some university experiments in which astrologers gave their dates of birth to other astrologers who then wrote them a personal birth chart. The first astrologers were then given this personal chart along with another two taken at random from other charts. Very few were able to recognise their own charts. I'd like to know if Dr Starr is aware of these experiments, they were carried out at the University of California I think.

B I would like to answer that question by telling listeners of an experiment I did in conjunction with the University of London, which proved conclusively that the two basic psychological attitudes of extroversion and introversion can be associated with alternate zodiac signs. Our experiments were replicated by world famous psychologists with the same success rate.

A Really? Well, we've just got time for one more question. I think we have another caller on line six now. Could we have your question please?

C4 Astrology doesn't seem to take into any account what we actually inherit from our parents, nor how our environment conditions our personality. It seems that if astrologists can predict our future then we have no free will as such.

A I'll just repeat that question for our listeners. The caller is saying that other things influence our character besides the position of the stars and that in any case if astrologers really can forecast our future this means we have no control over our life. Dr Starr?

B Obviously astrologers cannot predict every event, what kind of a life would it be if they could? Of course there is freedom of choice, but the framework within which these choices are made is part of a general trend which astrologers can and do predict.

A Thank you very much indeed Dr Starr, it's been most enlightening having you on the show tonight.

B Thank you.

1 Star signs

How typical are you of your sign? Try and guess which description refers to your sign.

Read 1-4: Aries (21 Mar – 20 Apr), Taurus (21 Apr – 20 May), Gemini (21 May – 21 June), Cancer (22 June – 22 July)

Read 5-8: Leo (23 July – 22 Aug), Virgo (23 Aug – 22 Sep), Libra (23 Sep – 22 Oct), Scorpio (23 Oct – 22 November)

Read 9-12: Sagittarius (23 Nov – 22 Dec), Capricorn (23 Dec – 20 Jan), Aquarius (21 Jan – 19 Feb), Pisces (20 Feb – 20 Mar)

1 Forceful; hate monotony; candid; single-minded; difficulty in controlling temper but not angry for long; impulsive; passionate lover; loyal; like red; resilient; try to run others' lives; money important for buying not for security.

2 Don't like routine; use hand gestures; often two-faced; not jealous; good at hiding true motives; interested in too many things; creative imagination; often late; need to communicate; gift for languages; enjoy flirting and need fantasy not just the physical.

3 Like money for security; like stable relationships; placid, patient and tolerant, unless pushed too far; unforgiving; possessive; attached to family and friends; sensuous; nature-lover; appreciate the arts; practical and reliable; like good food; good health; industrious; set in ways.

4 Family-oriented; prudent; seem self-confident but in reality sensitive; loving but need reassurance; reverence for the past; good memory; intuitive; easily influenced; loyal but like flirting; gregarious but need solitude; enjoy feeding others; imaginative.

5 Practical; neat; ambitious and hard working; care what others think about you; intellectual; critical and analytical mind; critical of others; dependable, strong sense of duty; constantly busy; a bit of a hypochondriac; worrier; conventional; excellent memory; shy in relationships.

6 Born leader, organise others' lives; pride and dignity if unchecked can become arrogance; need affection; love luxury, beauty, pleasure; warm and generous; exhibitionist; eat food in style; intolerant and dogmatic; good health; enjoy being centre of attention.

7 Like peace and harmony; see both sides of an argument; slow in making decisions and stubborn afterwards; need to share; like clean, beautiful environment; strong sense of justice; patient listener; fall in love with love; try to please people all the time; dislike conflict; eye for beauty; adaptable.

8 Forceful but not aggressive; deep intense thoughts and emotions; penetrating eyes; secretive; passionate about everything; want to be respected and control your life and others; say what you think; empathise with people; a little envious; sociable but like own company.

9 Ambitious; stoical and persistent; independent; faithful and keep promises; economical without being mean; love music; not romantic or sentimental; enjoy own company; responsible and dependable; like routine; a bit pessimistic; good organizer, good memory; practical and resourceful.

10 Honest, sincere and trusting; a little tactless; love travel and adventure; need freedom in relationships; idealist; like challenges; ready to take chances; like outdoor activities and sport; lucky, animal lover; optimistic, sunny nature.

11 Sociable; non-conformist; see through pretension; search to understand life and people; desire to experiment; devoted and faithful lover; need freedom in all spheres; love to communicate; analytical and questioning; humanitarian; imaginative and original; unpredictable, creative.

12 Idealist/dreamer; sensitive, easily hurt; wisdom of human nature; in love with love; need reassurance and encouragement; evasive; intuitive; aim to please everyone; tolerant; secretive; caring lover; imaginative.

2 Space research

- Tell students to mark the statements as true or false.

(i) (1) Space missions are not an end in themselves. Technology developed by NASA can monitor the earth's environment for potentially disruptive changes in climate and pollution levels. Satellites, for example, can pinpoint places which are good for fishing. A technology programme has been designed to help private companies capitalise on the lightweight materials and compact power systems produced by the space agency. Aircraft manufacturers are now looking into ways of developing planets that could fly passengers up to three times the speed of sound.   (3) & (5) These are common predictions made by such people Dr Arthur C. Clarke. (6) Ancient Greek philosophers, such as Democritus, often talked about such things.   (7) The Roman Catholic church used to say so, and maybe still does.

- Finally, use the extracts as a starting point for a short class debate on the subject of space research, and on whether the students themselves would be interested in visiting or colonising other planets.

3 Aliens and UFOs

- Refer students to the illustration of the UFO in **Space research** and ask them what UFO stands for (Unidentified Flying Object). As a whole class activity ask them the following questions: Do you believe in UFOs? Is belief in UFOs similar to beliefs in fairies, ghosts, visions and miracles? Can you think of any logical explanations for what people claim to have been UFOs? Does the fact that there have been considerably fewer UFO sightings since the Cold War ended indicate anything?
- Tell students that a UFO recently landed near the school. The alien passenger is doing an interplanetary survey on people's intelligence and habits in various parts of the universe. The students have been chosen, as examples of intelligent human life, to answer the alien's questions. Students discuss the questions in groups, with one person taking the part of the alien. Students don't need to answer all the questions, but they should all be read as they also relate to the rest of the listening exercise below.

Listening

- Students first hear an example of how to conduct the conversation and then role-play the conversation themselves. Play the tape as far as *.

(A = alien; S = student)

A We've heard that you have a strange force, called the police force — is that some kind of energy?

S No they're not an energetic force, but a group of people who protect you and your possessions.

A Protect you from who?

S Well, from criminals of course.

A Sorry, criminals? What are criminals?

S Criminals are people who break the law, you know, people who steal things, who attack you if they want something you've got or just because they don't like you.

A And you call this intelligent behaviour? We were led to believe that humans had reached a high level of intelligence.

S Er. Well. *

- Students then hear someone interviewing the alien. Students' task is to understand which questions on their page were asked, and how the alien answered.

9 *no doors – no heat loss, no stealing*   **5** *removable*   **1** *no colour discrimination, in fact no discrimination at all*   **8** *10 minutes' artificial sleep*   **7** *becoming smaller until they disappear*

S I'd like to begin by referring to your question on doors. I take it from your question that you don't have doors.

A There is absolutely no need for them. You told me that you need them to keep the heat in or out, but we can of course control the temperature on our planet. You also said you need them for protective purposes, to stop people stealing — the concept of stealing doesn't even exist on our planet, we have no word for it just as we have no word for 'truth', 'honesty' and 'law'.

S I can see why you asked us about wheels as I see you have some attached to your feet.

A They are of course removable by pressing the button behind our ears. We can also get instant flippers for travelling underwater, or wings for flying.

S Wonderful. Are you all green?

A Yes.

S Isn't that a bit boring?

A Maybe. But at least there's no colour discrimination. In fact there cannot be any discrimination as we're all the same. Same size, same age, same intelligence. The only thing that's not the same the different sexes. I could easily say: 'Isn't just having two sexes boring?', but I won't because I'm too intelligent for that.

S I'm curious to know about sleep.

A What a wasteful idea. Do you realise that you humans spend about a third of your life in bed? We merely go into an artificial sleep room, where in ten minutes we can renew our energies. We thus have a much fuller life than you, especially as we live forever.

S You mean you're immortal. So how do you manage with overpopulation and feeding so many people?

A We're not exactly immortal. Eventually we will actually disappear. You see as our numbers increase, we decrease in size.

S What do you mean? You physically shrink?

A That's right. Every year the government decides on how much smaller we need to be. But that doesn't just apply to us as living creatures, but all that surrounds us. So as we get smaller so do our houses, our cars, everything in fact, including the vegetation. Eventually of course we will get so small as to become invisible.

S Why don't you just make your planet bigger?

A What an excellent idea! We hadn't thought about that. Maybe you humans are intelligent after all!

2 Space research

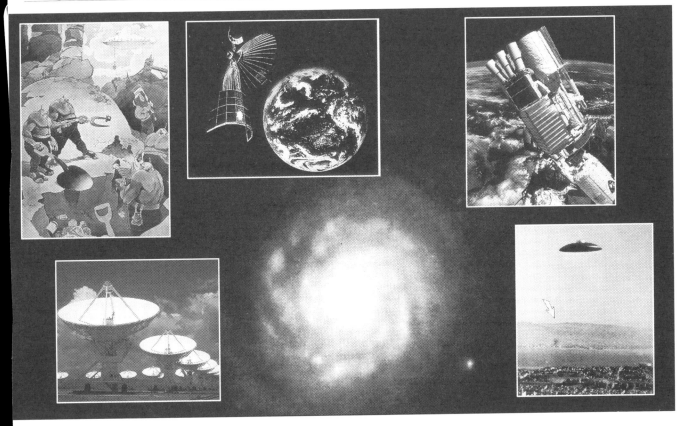

1 Sending rockets, people and satellites into space is a waste of money – we do not need a space programme.

2 Trying to discover new, and possibly hospitable, planets is vital for our future survival.

3 Soon intercontinental aeroplanes will travel at three times the speed of sound.

4 What were considered science fiction films twenty years ago would now be considered reflections of reality.

5 In 400 years we will probably have colonised Mars.

6 It's only in the last hundred years that we have begun to believe that we may not be alone in the universe.

7 Life on earth is unique and was created by a divine act. It is heretical to talk about the possibility of alien life.

8 If there is a God, then this God will be the ruler of aliens too.

3 Aliens and UFOs

> Intelligent life in the universe? Guaranteed. Intelligent life in our galaxy? So overwhelmingly likely that I'd give you almost any odd you'd like.

(Paul Horowitz of the Search for Extra-Terrestrial Intelligence unit at Harvard University.)

1 Why aren't you all green?

2 Why are there only two sexes?

3 Why don't you all speak the same language?

4 Why do you have ten fingers?

5 Why don't you have wheels?

6 Why do you wear clothes?

7 How do you cope with population increase?

8 Why do you sleep?

9 Why do buildings have doors?

10 Why do you grow old?

Score:

Intelligence rating: zero, sub-normal, normal, super

Subject Index

Capital letter and number refers to unit title and exercise, * = listening exercise, w = warm-up, e = extra, f = follow up